RIF
Reading Is Fundamental
THIS BOOK BELONGS TO:

Disneynature

AFRICAN CATS

Photography credits:
Owen Newman: 6, 10, 12-13, 15, 26-27, 28-29, 30-31, 32, 33, 34-35, 36, 37, 57, 58, 60-61, 62, 65, 66, 67, 74, 93, 94, 95, 96, 97, 98, 99, 104, 111, 112-113, 114, 123, 124, 125, 126, 127,128-129, 130, 132-133, 143, 144, 146, 150, 152-153, 164-165, 167, 168-169, 170, 177, 178, 188-189, 190, 192, 193, 194, 197, 200, 201, 206-207
Keith Scholey: 16, 18-19, 21, 23, 38, 41, 42-43, 45, 47, 48-49, 50, 52, 53, 55-56, 69, 70-71, 72, 73, 76, 78-79, 80, 81, 83, 84, 85, 88-89, 107, 108, 109, 117, 118, 119, 135, 136, 137, 139, 141, 145, 154, 156 (top), 158, 159, 160, 173, 174, 175, 183, 184, 185, 201, 202
Natasha Breed: 101, 102-103, 147, 162, 186, 200, 201
David Breed: 149, 156 (bottom)
Oliver Scholey: 87, 140
Simon King: 201, 202
Marguerite Smits van Oyen: 22
Sophie Darlington: 202

Illustrated by Jean-Paul Orpiñas
Designed by Stuart Smith

For information address Disney Editions, 114 Fifth Avenue, New York, New York 10011-5690.

Printed in United States of America
First Edition
10 9 8 7 6 5 4 3 2 1
ISBN: 9781423134107
F322-8368-0-11001

DISNEYNATURE PRESENTS "AFRICAN CATS" A BIG CAT PRODUCTION MUSIC BY NICHOLAS HOOPER PRODUCED BY KEITH SCHOLEY AND ALIX TIDMARSH DIRECTED BY KEITH SCHOLEY AND ALASTAIR FOTHERGILL

Disneynature

AFRICAN CATS

THE STORY BEHIND THE FILM

BY AMANDA BARRETT AND KEITH SCHOLEY

Disney
EDITIONS
NEW YORK

TABLE OF CONTENTS

PART THREE 120

We knew that behind every big cat lies a great story—even so, we had no idea just how many twists and turns would be revealed in their tales.

INTRODUCTION

We have just spent two incredible years with cheetahs and lions in the Masai Mara while making the Disneynature film, *African Cats*. Though we are experts in filming big cats, even we hadn't been able to spend such a long time with individual animals before, and the opportunity gave us unparalleled insight into their lives. We shot hundreds of hours of tape before distilling the chaos and complexity of their world into a film that lasts just over an hour. Now, this book gives us a welcome chance to share in greater detail our emotional roller-coaster ride of suspense and drama. The events took place between August 2008 and September 2010, and they show that in the lives of these African cats, truth really is stranger than fiction.

Amanda Barrett
Keith Scholey

October 2010

PART ONE

OLD FRIENDS

It's a windy morning on the African plains in early April 2010, and the sun is shining brightly on long, yellow grasses bending double in the breeze. The canopy of a tree casts a tiny pool of cooling shadows, and tightly packed in the shifting, leaf-dappled shade, with paws resting on bellies, several young lions sleep peacefully. Safari cars arrive, and tourists take quick snapshots before the cars and their passengers drive off again on a quest to find a rhino or buffalo. To these people, the lions are a great but brief photographic opportunity. To us, they are old friends, each with a story to tell of trial, tribulation, and triumph. In the last two years, their world has been our world, and we have often lived in apprehension not knowing what will happen to them next. Before the end of the month, we have to bid the lions a fond farewell though, of course, they'll be oblivious to the occasion. And although we can now do justice to the tale of their early years, the next chapter in their lives will, sadly, remain unwritten.

OPPOSITE PAGE: After all their trials and tribulations, we felt like proud parents as the young males grew up and began to grow short, punk-like manes and "mutton-chop" whiskers.

PAGES 12–13: After following this group of young lions for seventeen months, we thought of them as old friends.

When we as a team first met these lions, they were large, clumsy cubs, part of a big pride whose home range encompassed the thickly wooded area around the Ndonya Oseiya hills in Kenya's Masai Mara National Reserve.

A lion pride consists of adult females, all of them related to each other as mothers, sisters, aunts, daughters, or nieces. While lionesses try to stay in the same area, handing down prime locations to their female offspring, adult males live different lives. Pushed out by their parents, young males roam far and wide trying to find a place to settle. If they're lucky, they will find a pride of females without any resident males. At this point, a small coalition of two or three male lions will tend to stay with one pride. But occasionally, bigger coalitions of males band together and may continue to prowl back and forth between different prides of females, rarely settling with one group for any length of time. However, all adult males have one purpose: to father cubs and ensure that these cubs survive long enough to stand a chance of passing on their father's genes.

Each individual lion has a different personality, possesses different skills, and plays a different role in the overall health of the pride. The success of a pride depends on the adult females' ability to hunt and whether the pride males can keep intruding males at bay long enough to raise their cubs to maturity. In this way, luck, both good and bad, has its own part to play. And, over time, the strength of a pride will wax and wane in the same way human empires rise and fall.

If we were going to reveal how a pride's fortunes are open to the vagaries of chance, as we already knew, we had to find the right lions for *African Cats*. And from the start of our project in August 2008, part of the challenge was finding a pride whose home range didn't include the international boundary dividing Kenya and Tanzania. A simple line of concrete posts across a wide, rolling grassy plain demarcates the frontier between the two African countries, so crossing the international border is easy for animals, but since there's no formal border checkpoint close by, crossing from the Kenyan reserve into Tanzania's Serengeti National Park was impossible for people such as us.

In some years, up to 600,000 wildebeests migrate into Kenya to spend four-to-five months grazing the long grasses in the Masai Mara National Reserve.

In our first three months, we marveled at the spectacle of the wildebeest herds, the beautiful misty mornings, heat-hazy afternoons, and dramatic storms; but finding the "right" lion pride was harder than we'd imagined since most of them disappeared over the Kenyan/Tanzanian border sooner or later. So we started to focus elsewhere, moving into the heart of the reserve, below a range of hills known as Ndonya Oseiya where the Mara River loops its way through the plains and woodland in gentle curves and tight, sinuous bends.

The Masai Mara National Reserve is the northern offshoot of the Serengeti ecosystem. "Ecosystem" is a simple word to describe the rolling grassy plains, wooded valleys, rivers, and thickets that make up a landscape of priceless beauty and one of the most intact savanna systems left on earth. Home to an almost bewildering mix of animals—including buffalo, elephants, giraffes, and antelope.

For a few months every year, it's also a meeting place for the Loita Plains wildebeests and zebras who move in from the north. These combine with huge zebra herds and, in some years, almost half of the total population of 1,300,000 Serengeti wildebeests moving up from the south. With such an abundance of prey, this place, we thought, must be paradise on earth for lions.

OPPOSITE PAGE: Impalas are one of the many species of resident antelope that live in the Masai Mara all year round.

PAGES 18–19: Giraffes cross the open plains searching for thorn trees, which provide almost all of their sustenance.

Finding the right lion pride was a struggle. In contrast, finding our other main character, the cheetah, almost fell into our laps. From the start, we planned to follow a cheetah family alongside a lion pride because a cheetah's life is very different from a lion's, despite her also being a big cat. Cheetahs have no pride for security. The females are solitary, and so when cheetah mothers raise cubs, everything rests on them as leaders. For us, finding a cheetah mother with cubs was essential for the film.

As we arrived in the Mara in August 2008, a small miracle was taking place just a few kilometers from our base camp north of the Mara River. A cheetah had given birth to six cubs. At this very tender stage, cubs are totally blind, weigh only ten ounces, and remain hidden in a grassy den. It was a lucky break for us, though at that point, we had little idea just how much this cheetah mother would impact all of our lives during the next two years.

Most people know that cheetahs are the fastest cats, but fewer are aware that this makes them particularly vulnerable. In order to achieve speed, they have sacrificed strength, and the result is that they are bullied by most other large carnivores. Getting to keep and eat what they catch is the cheetah's problem. Their plight intensifies when they have cubs. It is this vulnerability that makes a cheetah's story so powerful, especially in the Masai Mara, a place full of dangerous animals.

Statistics from the neighboring Serengeti show that only one in twenty cheetah cubs survives to the age of independence—around eighteen months. Hyenas, jackals, pythons, and others all play a part in this phenomenon, but lions appear to be the main culprits. Having followed many young cheetah families in the past, we knew that this was likely to be a heartrending experience, with tragedy almost inevitable. But following this cheetah and her newborns had to be our goal, and there was always the hope that it would result in a happy ending.

Many cheetahs roam the plains of the Mara, but finding one who had just given birth to a litter of cubs was a rarity.

Would this cheetah prove to be the right choice for our leading cheetah character? Ultimately, that would hinge on her ability to raise her cubs. Only time would tell, but at first, her success was a long shot. The den where these cubs would spend the first weeks of their lives was ominously close to a shallow riverine gully called the Bila Shaka lugga, the heart of one of the Mara's most powerful lion pride's territory. That the den was in a dangerous location was not surprising, as there is no safe haven in a place like the Masai Mara, where the number of predators is so high. However, the Bila Shaka pride was perhaps the greatest threat of all. The Mara predators are extremely competitive, and given the chance would kill each other. A blind ten-ounce cheetah cub detected by a 500-pound Bila Shaka lion would hardly stand a chance.

OPPOSITE PAGE: Blind, defenseless, and vulnerable to predators, these cubs spent the first six weeks of their lives hidden in a small grassy den.

ABOVE: Cheetahs are the fastest land mammal in the world, but they lack the strength of other African cats and hold a weak position in the hierarchy of the plains.

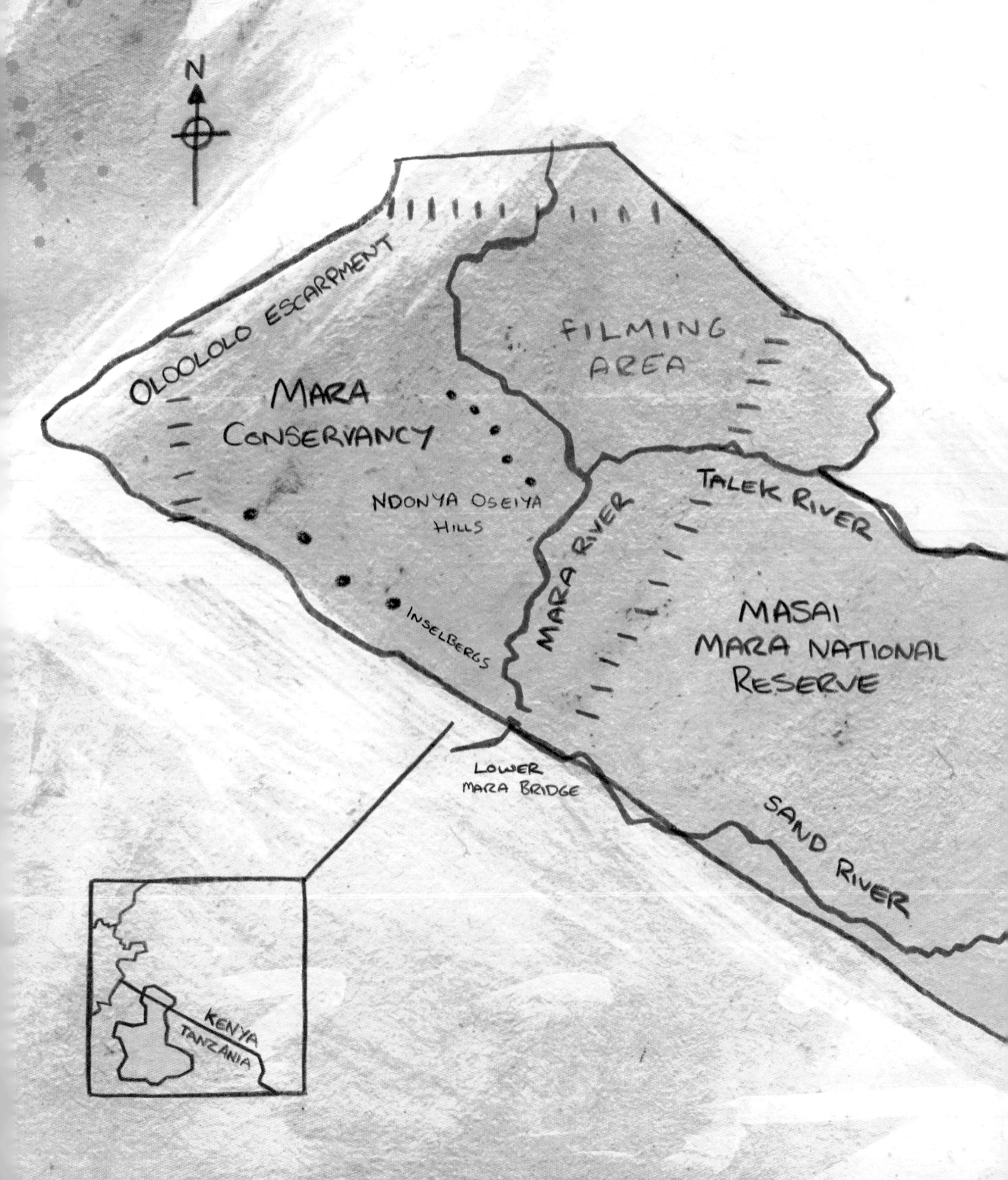
N
OLOOLOLO ESCARPMENT
FILMING AREA
MARA CONSERVANCY
NDONYA OSEIYA HILLS
INSELBERGS
MARA RIVER
TALEK RIVER
MASAI MARA NATIONAL RESERVE
LOWER MARA BRIDGE
SAND RIVER
KENYA
TANZANIA

How is it that cheetahs and lions can still be found in such abundance in this African haven? A little more than a century ago, the Mara had no boundaries and was part of a huge wilderness that stretched across eastern Africa. Then, just the Maasai tribesmen, a nomadic pastoral people who relied upon their cows for existence, lived here along with the numerous wild animals around them. As the twentieth century dawned, the Mara became part of the Kenya colony of the expanding British Empire, and then part of independent Kenya in the 1960s, and the Mara and its Maasai inhabitants remained almost untouched by the political change. Even in colonial times, the importance of the Mara as a crucial wildlife area became recognized along with the huge Serengeti on its border in Tanzania, and both subsequently became protected areas. After independence, Kenya's Masai Mara became a national game reserve, an area still owned by the Maasai people but set aside as an area for the protection of wildlife. With 1,510 square kilometers of protected land, the Masai Mara is similar in structure to a national park but administered and run by local county councils.

Although human politics are critical in determining whether or not the African cats have a long-term future, for the cats themselves it has been the same battle for survival for millennia. At the start of our filming, it seemed almost unthinkable that our cheetah cubs could survive this battle, exposed as they were in their grassy den. We had found our cheetahs—for now. And it was time to find our lion pride, too.

PAGES 26–29: Wildebeest herds have an uncanny knack for anticipating the rains and arrive in huge numbers ready to take advantage of the freshly growing grasses.

Early in November 2008, we still hadn't found a lion pride on which to focus and were wondering if we should move on yet again. Then on November 17, about twelve kilometers from our camp, we found a group of large lion cubs sitting up, looking around nervously. They seemed all alone amid long, dry grasses that almost hid them from sight. Suddenly a lioness appeared, and after a warm greeting with the cubs, who ecstatically rubbed their heads and bodies under her chin, she took them on a journey down a grassy slope, through a gully, and into a small valley right on the edge of the Mara River. We followed close behind and along the way, a magnificent male lion with a huge black mane joined the throng.

The lions traveled more than two kilometers before making a beeline for a group of other females feeding on a freshly killed zebra. We stopped to catch our breath and start counting. The final tally numbered nineteen lions. We'd followed a female with eight large youngsters. Then there was the male and five other females. Of these, one was an elderly lioness with a young cub, about six months old, hugging her side. Another was a younger female with three tiny cubs that she was guarding protectively from the older, more boisterous youngsters.

It was now that we noticed that the male had a lower canine tooth split in half vertically, with one half flopping down outside his lip. It looked unbelievably painful but, surprisingly, seemed to cause him little trouble as he tugged and pulled the zebra carcass. The older lioness with the six-month-old cub had injuries too, including a large wound on her back. We weren't sure about the origin of this wound, but females fight females from other prides in order to protect their land, and sometimes they're forced to attack intruding males to save their cubs. Often in such encounters, lions try to paralyze each other by biting deep down into the base of the spine. Whatever battles she'd waged, the results were that her hind legs were pitifully thin, and it was clear that she found it difficult to put her weight on one front leg.

This lioness and her cub caught our attention and soon both became the major "lion stars" of the film.

ABOVE: The three youngest cubs in the pride were about two months old.

OPPOSITE PAGE: The male was very distinctive with a lower canine that had split in half vertically.

The eight large cubs kept together in a tight little bunch. We reckoned they were about ten or eleven months old, so they were totally dependent on the females to catch food. They'd been weaned for about six months, and none of them showed any close associations with any of the four females that could have been their mothers. It was intriguing to think who might be the son or daughter of whom, and with such a great mix of lions of so many different ages, we felt our leonine red-letter day had finally arrived. The next challenge was whether we'd be able to find them regularly enough to watch their story unfold.

Cheetahs are generally active from soon after sunrise to sunset but lions, more often than not, do relatively little during the day, moving into the shade of thickets by mid-morning and staying still for the rest of the day. This can make them almost impossible to find, but for the following three weeks, we got lucky and found the pride almost every day. Though they were rarely all together in a group, they were often within eyesight of each other. This gave us the chance to look at the shapes of their faces and bodies and work out some of the family resemblances between a few of the larger cubs and one or two of the adult females.

We also started to be able to tell the adult females apart. The limping lioness was instantly recognizable, but for the others, the only foolproof way was to look closely at their whisker spots. On either side of their noses, all lions have three regular rows of whisker spots. On top of these regular rows is another line with irregular spots. This irregular row is matched to the regular line of six or seven whisker spots below. Using these as reference, the irregular spots on the top row are counted working outward from the nose. These irregular spots are unique to each lion and stay the same for life.

Once we knew who was who, we began to notice different personalities and behavior. One female would normally instigate hunting while a different one would be more patient in stalking, and yet another was good at running. In this way, they could work together as a great team. From there, it just depended if they were in the right place at the right time. Sometimes one would stalk into position and wait patiently for the others to join her before turning around to see the others still snoozing where she'd left them. None of the lionesses were dominant, and cooperative hunting in the classic sense seemed to be a rare event. Some of the lionesses seemed to be less reliable than others, almost as though they were simply fair-weather friends.

We found out that one of the pride's favorite places was a series of tiny rocky outcrops overlooking the Mara River. We called it Headquarters One, since from up here the lions seemed to be regally surveying the lands below them. The weather was glorious with long, sunny days and barely a hint of wind. Most of the lions were eating well, and it seemed they didn't have a care in the world.

We started giving them names, sometimes inspired by the obvious. The male was "Fang." We had thought another male or two might turn up, but as the days passed, it became obvious that Fang was the only adult male in the group, a position that made him quite unusual in the reserve. And there was another anomaly: a female with three tiny cubs living on the

periphery of the pride. She was often in sight of the pride, and though none of the females chased her away, neither she nor the others ever moved closer. She could have been a niece, sister, or daughter, but her face looked so similar to the limping lioness that we hazarded a guess she was a sister or daughter. Looking at her nose helped us decide her likely age. As lions get older, their young, bright pink noses slowly become freckled with black until, in the end, there's hardly any pink left.

The injured lioness's nose was almost black while the unknown female's was bright pink with tiny freckles of black, so we thought it was possible that they were mother and daughter. Since the daughter lived on the outskirts of the pride, we borrowed the Latin word for "moon" and called her Luna.

In Arabic, "layla" means dark beauty, and since a hint of tragedy clung to the limping lioness, this became her name. Her cub was a little female with what seemed, to us, a habitually anxious expression. And no wonder. One of her mother's front legs was giving her lots of trouble and though it didn't look broken or swollen, on some days she could barely move. As a result, Layla could rarely keep up with the pride, and she and the cub were often alone. They were far thinner than the others, and a slight worry we had from the outset increased as we wondered what would happen to them in the next few weeks?

PAGE 34: One of the rare occasions when most of the pride were sitting together at Headquarters One.

ABOVE and OPPOSITE PAGE: Luna and her cub were, we thought, Layla's daughter and granddaughter though they were outcasts from the pride.

There were uncertainties and mysteries with the cheetah family too. The cheetah mother had given birth to six cubs, so we decided to call her Sita, which means "six" in Swahili. We first saw Sita when she was hunting out on the plains, far away from the den, having temporarily abandoned the cubs while she looked for food. She looked as beautiful as cheetahs come, perfectly proportioned and without a blemish on her spotted, furry coat. What her appearance did not reveal was that we were looking at the most courageous animal we were ever likely to follow. We were going to have to learn that through her actions. We would have shuddered, too, if we'd had even a tiny inkling of what the next few months would bring. At that point she was still just another cheetah.

We had been following cheetahs in this area for more than a decade, making, since 1996, a series of television wildlife films called *Big Cat Diary*. So although we had given her a new name, Sita may well have been a cheetah we had known in the past. This would be important to figure out. Was she a new mother, or experienced at raising cubs? If a cheetah mother is inexperienced, the odds of survival for her cubs are slim. New mothers tend not to be alert enough to the dangers around them, and are yet to learn how to deal with trouble when it arises. It is heart-wrenching to witness inexperienced cheetah mothers lose their cubs so quickly. Although cheetahs learn from their mistakes, for a mother there is no greater mistake than losing a cub. If we could learn Sita's history, we would have a far better idea of the chances that she would be able to raise cubs to adulthood.

Like lions, female cheetahs appear superficially very similar, and identifying them is a painstaking task. Fortunately, the process is easier than with lions because each cheetah has unique spot patterns on its coat, in much the same way our fingerprints are unique. We chose to use the spot pattern on the face, where it is clearest and because we had kept sketches of the faces of all the Mara cheetahs we had followed over the years. It was a very exciting moment when we discovered that one cheetah sketch appeared to match Sita's spot pattern. We had previously known this cheetah as "Duma's mother." Duma, named after the Swahili word for "cheetah," was a small cub that we had followed in 2004, along with her mother who was the cheetah that we were now calling Sita. So our Sita was an old cheetah—at least seven years old as we started filming in 2008—and we knew that she had already raised at least one cub to adulthood. However, not all of her cubs had been so lucky. While filming

PAGE 38: Every cheetah has a unique spot pattern on its coat which can be used to identify it.

OPPOSITE PAGE, TOP: Cheetahs are not a threat to buffalo, as they are far too big for a cheetah to hunt. Yet despite this, buffalo will attack cheetahs as they are wary of any big cat. For a cheetah with small cubs, buffalo are a perilous beast.

OPPOSITE PAGE, BOTTOM: Having lost one cub in the den, Sita kept her five remaining cubs close to her.

PAGES 42–43: For Sita, sunrise was a good sign. Night was a dangerous time, as lions, hyenas, and other predators took advantage of the cooler temperatures to go on the prowl.

another project in 2005, we had again come across Sita who had, tragically, just lost an entire litter of cubs. Our newborn cubs' fate now rested on whether Sita had learned the lessons of her previous tragedies. Sita had experience, but would it be enough?

As we reacquainted ourselves with Sita, our emotional attachment grew. It is a wonderful time when you start to spend day after day with a wild animal and really get to know it. At first, Sita was like an "interesting neighbor," but she quickly became a devoted best friend, and almost family. Every night in camp, Sita and the cubs would usually end up being the topic of conversation for the cheetah crew. "Is she hunting enough?" "Are those lions getting too close?" "Is that little cub with the white tuft on its tail sick?" We started to worry about the family, and while most of our worries proved unnecessary, some of our fears unfortunately had merit.

One night, in the distance, an ominous herd of buffalo slowly drifted toward the den. Buffalo may be grass-eaters rather than predators, but any Maasai tribesman will tell you that they are the most dangerous animals on the plains. Cheetahs are far too small to cause any harm to these enormous animals, but lions hunt buffalo, causing buffalo to be nervous around any cat, be it a lion, leopard, or cheetah. If a buffalo senses a cheetah nearby, it may charge toward the cheetah to drive it off. Any cubs near the cheetah could be trampled, or worse, targeted and gored to death on the buffalo's horns: a tragic outcome for a cheetah family who posed no threat to the buffalo herd.

We will never know for sure what happened on the plains of the Mara that night. The following morning, we found Sita awake, agitated, and calling. Only five cubs could be seen. The buffalo herd was still close by, so all we could presume was that one of the cubs had been separated or trampled in the night. It was a sad day, but we were also relieved. There was a real risk that none of the cubs might have made it through the night, and thankfully, five survived. It was a sharp reminder of the dangers ahead. As with the lions, following Sita and her cubs was going to stretch our emotional capacities.

At four weeks old, cheetah cubs feed entirely from their mother's milk, and with five rapidly growing cubs, Sita needed to produce large amounts each day. To do this, she had to keep herself well fed, and so every other day she set off hunting.

But hunting was risky, as it meant leaving the den unguarded. Fortunately, Sita could rest assured that, in the heat of the day, most other predators were fast asleep. Hunting, under the hot African sun, is strenuous, but cheetahs specialize in hunting at this time of day. As the least powerful and most vulnerable of the large predators, Sita might make a kill at night, but it would likely be taken from her by lions or hyenas. Worse still, her cubs would be in far greater danger if they were left alone around nighttime while other predators were active. So, as heat haze blurred the air in the blistering ninety-five degree heat, and the Bila Shaka lions lay asleep under the shade of a Balanites tree, Sita would set off from the den in search of prey. Following a cheetah on the hunt takes commitment, as it may be a day or two before she succeeds. But it is one of the most gripping events to witness, with both predator and prey in a life-and-death struggle. Watching a chase always pulled us in many conflicting directions—from fear and deep sympathy for Sita's prey to intense worry for Sita and her cubs when she failed.

For Sita, hunting was a laborious undertaking. She often had to trek for kilometers to find prey—often a gazelle—all the while pausing at vantage points to scan the horizon for potential danger. Cheetahs rarely select large herds of gazelles, since if just one spots the stalking cheetah, it will alert the entire herd. Instead, cheetahs will scour the plains for lone gazelles, usually male Thomson's gazelles, as they often graze alone.

Once Sita had spotted a potential gazelle, she would stare at it for ages, maybe to judge if the gazelle was fit, injured, or pregnant. If it was in any way hindered, Sita would charge the gazelle from a large distance and still catch it with relative ease. However, with most fit gazelles, she needed to work out how close she could stalk toward it. Often, we would watch in bemusement

Elephants are abundant across the Masai Mara. Their constant browsing on thorn trees and young seedlings helps to maintain large areas of the Mara as open grassland—ideal habitat for cheetahs and their gazelle prey.

as Sita would just walk off in the other direction, having stared at a gazelle for half an hour. Clearly, she had figured out that she would never be able to get close enough and was not going to waste her energy trying. Experienced cheetahs are very good at making these judgments.

So when Sita finally committed to a hunt, she nearly always succeeded. Cheetahs have to get good; wasting energy is a true killer of predators. If poor judgment results in failure, the cheetah will become weaker and as a result, fail more. It is a vicious cycle that leads to starvation, which in Sita's case would be bad news for both she and her cubs. Luck also plays a part in survival. One poor foothold can lead to a trip, a fall, an injury, and ultimately the end of six cheetah lives.

When Sita judges her chances to be good, she enters into the final stages of the hunt. She leaves her vantage point for lower ground and starts to stalk through the long grass, which conceals most of her body. If the gazelle has its head down, Sita moves quickly, but she freezes like a statue if the gazelle looks up. Slowly, Sita closes the gap. This stage of the hunt is very tense. Sometimes, the cheetah seems so close to the gazelle that you cannot understand why she does not charge. But the timing of her run is her most crucial decision. She must go at top speed and that costs her much energy, so she has to judge the situation perfectly. Her success rate must be high.

Suddenly, all that tension explodes into a heart-stopping and frenetic chase. The sound is incredible, with noises as loud, wild, and powerful as those of a galloping horse. Quite possibly, the gazelle hears Sita before seeing her. Either way, for a gazelle, it must be the sound from hell. When the chase begins, Sita closes in on the gazelle rapidly, but as the gazelle accelerates, the two become more evenly matched. Once the gazelle realizes that the cheetah is beginning to overwhelm it, it starts violently shifting direction in an attempt to outmaneuver the cheetah. This defense is often successful against lions, but cheetahs like Sita are too agile, and so she continues to close in on the gazelle. Then, when the gazelle is within reach, Sita deftly trips her prey with her forepaw, sending it tumbling to the ground. As it falls, Sita locks her jaws around the gazelle's throat, quickly suffocating it to death.

Hunts always produce mixed emotions. If the hunt is successful, a gazelle dies, which is obviously hard to watch. Yet, if Sita failed to make a kill for too long, she and her cubs would starve. The modern world tends to shelter us from this aspect of life, but it becomes brutally apparent on the African plains. While grappling with ideas of life and death, one cannot help but be in awe of the cheetah's power, speed, and agility. There is little we have ever witnessed, be it natural or man-made, that is as breathtaking as a cheetah chase. No matter how many cheetah chases you see, you remember every one.

OPPOSITE PAGE, TOP: Sita had to stalk to within thirty meters of a gazelle, all the while taking pains to go undetected.

OPPOSITE PAGE, BOTTOM: Sita could stalk for as long as half an hour. If a nearby animal noticed her and gave an alarm call, her game would be up. Then Sita would walk away, still hungry, with her time and energy having gone to waste.

Each chase was fraught with danger. Sita had less than a minute to catch the gazelle before becoming exhausted. If she failed, the wasted energy would make her next attempt even more of a struggle. Injury was also a risk. Running at full speed, a trip could be life-threatening. Equally, the gazelle could seriously hurt Sita, so she killed her prey immediately upon catching it.

The cubs we had found with Sita soon grew too old to feed solely from her milk. At six weeks old, they needed to eat meat. One morning, Sita left the den to hunt as usual, but this time she called for her cubs to follow. The cubs seemed to relish their first steps across the African plains, bounding along with abandon and gazing in awe at their spectacular surroundings. But Sita was far from playing with abandon. She looked nervous and was constantly alert, often pausing to scan the horizon and nearby bushes for any sign of danger. Through bitter experience, Sita must have learned just how dangerous the Mara can be. Yet the cubs were not in fear of the Masai Mara's dangers. They seemed exhilarated by their new environment and, for the time being, still unaware of its perils.

The most risky time of day came when Sita had to hunt. When she spotted a gazelle and began to stalk, the cubs recognized this as a signal for them not to follow her. The five cubs huddled together, completely exposed on the grassy plain, without their mother to watch for danger or protect them. The cubs, at this age, were so small and vulnerable that even large birds of prey, like the antelope-hunting martial eagle, could snatch them. It was always worrisome to watch these little fur balls, huddled together in the grass and left alone, as their mother walked away. At least we knew that their mother was an excellent huntress, rarely failing to provide their meal. As long as she remained fit, starvation was unlikely for this family.

Sita would spend most of her time around her cubs, where she was able to protect them from the many threats that the wilderness might pose.

Some speculate that there is one extra thing protecting cheetah cubs as they huddle together. At this young age, the fur on their bodies is darkish, apart from a layer of white, fluffy fur on their backs. This makes them look strikingly similar to honey badgers who, despite their rather cute name, are perhaps the most aggressive small carnivores on the plains. Honey badgers can attack anything, including humans. They have even been known to charge safari cars, and while these small animals have little hope of inflicting any serious damage on the car, seeing them viciously snarling as they charge forward is nonetheless alarming. Quite possibly, animals that would otherwise attack and kill these defenseless cheetah cubs are deterred from doing so, wrongly thinking that they are looking at a ferocious and maniacal honey badger.

Regardless, it still made us nervous to watch the cubs left alone. Once Sita made a kill, she either called for her cubs to join her or dragged the carcass back to them. It was always a relief when they were reunited, as Sita could at least guard the cubs. But the family was still in danger. The kill could attract lions and hyenas, so secrecy was vital to the cheetahs at this point, with them going to great lengths to make sure they were not noticed. Cheetahs have a high-pitched call that sounds more like a bird than a big cat, meaning that any noise they make is less likely to attract the attention of their enemies. Cheetahs also eat fast, and then quickly abandon the carcass to scavengers. So Sita was able to make sure that her cubs were not close to food for a moment longer than necessary. Well fed, the family then marched on, continuing its never-ending journey, looking for potential meals while trying to avoid ambush.

OPPOSITE PAGE: The martial eagle is one of Africa's largest birds of prey, usually hunting hares and small antelope. It can pose a threat to small cheetah cubs exposed on the plains.

ABOVE: The cubs were still too young to accompany Sita on hunts. So when Sita was finding their next meal, the cubs were left alone, for as long as an hour, vulnerable and exposed on the open plains.

PAGES 54–55: Sunset is a time of magical change, as the creatures of the night awaken and come out onto the plains.

Unlike Sita and her cubs, the lion pride stayed in one place, and for good reason. During the end of November and the beginning of December, the rocks and thickets around Headquarters One were, for lions, some of the best places to reside. Long lines of zebras were on the move out of the reserve, heading northeast to the fresh grass on the Loita Plains. Before leaving, however, they had to cross the Mara River, and this was a daunting proposition. The tumbling waters not only hid rocks and boulders but also large numbers of crocodiles in the calmer stretches. These are some of the largest, most powerful creatures in all of Africa. In addition, they are expert at lurking almost out of sight and staying motionless so they usually look more like innocent floating logs than fearsome predators.

But zebras are no fools and choose their crossing points carefully; and one of their favorites for several kilometers turned out to be a stretch of rapids below the rocky outcrops of Headquarters One. As the herds milled nervously in the bushes and reeds bordering the banks of the river, plucking up courage to cross, the lionesses would seize the opportunity to sneak off the rocks or out of the bushes and creep through the grasses below, before sometimes jumping on a zebra. Often, right at the last moment, they would appear to lose their nerve. We could sympathize, since a full-grown zebra is a heavy animal with a powerful kick and strong bite. Even catching the weaker foals is tricky since stallions fight hard on behalf of their herd.

While the pride was finding food, Layla's injury was getting worse. Many times, she was hobbling far behind the others, her cub looking tense and anxious beside her. However, Layla would do her best to catch up, and several times she showed us just how determined she could be. On one occasion, she could barely walk and yet, hours later, she eventually caught up with them. Amazingly, just afterward, she ran at top speed for more than 200 meters to separate a zebra foal from its herd. Another female cut in from a different direction to grab the foal, but without Layla's tremendous effort, the catch would have never been made. After the run, Layla was exhausted and in great pain. Unable to move, she lay in the shade watching while the other lions, including her cub, ate. Hours later, it was heartbreaking to see her stumble to her feet to chew a few tiny bones, all that was left after the rest had eaten their fill.

Fang often took the lion's share of any food, but he had a vital role to play in the protection of Layla's small cub as well as the three tiniest cubs of all. Not only that, we learned from the rangers that he had a sad history. Only a few months earlier, Fang had been part of a coalition of three males,

but one had sickened and died while the other had disappeared, and that was why Fang was all alone. If he relaxed his guard, disappeared, or died, intruding males would kill the cubs. Then, when the females came into estrus, they would mate with the intruders and give birth to their cubs. If the intruding males waited for the existing cubs to reach maturity, the lionesses might not come into estrus for a whole two years. Most male lions are four or five years old before they've got the strength, temerity, and muscle power to take over the pride. And by the time they're seven or eight, their strength is waning or they've lost their partners, and meanwhile, the next wave of usurping males is waiting in the wings. So it's important for these lions to act quickly once they've taken over a pride, otherwise their genes might not get passed onto the next generation.

Male lions with three or more members in a coalition tend to be winners rather than losers. Fang was now vulnerable, and if intruding males took over, they wouldn't just kill the four youngest cubs. The group of eight ten-to-eleven-month-old youngsters would be in danger as well. All of these, females and males, would be chased, injured, and eventually killed. The young females in this group wouldn't become sexually mature until they were about two and one-half years old, when they'd be valuable to the intruding males and, thus, safer. But the male youngsters had even longer to go. Sometimes, male cubs hang around their mothers, aunts, and sisters until they're three or even four. Fang's protection and his own welfare were vital to so many that, every morning, we hoped to find him with the pride.

Sometimes he'd be missing for a day or two, and we'd become increasingly anxious thinking he'd been killed or injured in a fight the night before. And then we'd find him kilometers away, patrolling his boundaries. We took comfort from the fact that lions tend to avoid fighting since even the victor can sustain major damage. Instead of a violent battle, lions roar to demonstrate to their neighbors just how strong and powerful they are. Fang was a master in this art, and one morning he gave such a thrilling performance that we remember it still.

Weak sunlight shone onto thick banks of mist that hung over the river. The air was chill, and there wasn't a breath of wind. Fang stared intently at something off in the distance without blinking or turning away.

Minutes later, he grumbled in a growling sort of way, coughed once or twice, then lowered his head and began to roar, again and again. The sound built, the bass notes rumbled, and his whole body shook, straining with the effort of making his voice heard across valley, hill, and river. He subsided into low coughs and then stopped, lifting his head back up to listen. A minute or so later, there was a faint answering roar that floated back across the river. He called in response again, and then Layla and the five other females

PAGE 57: The pride would often be content to watch the zebras as they passed by peacefully.

OPPOSITE PAGE, TOP: The survival of Layla's cub depended on Fang keeping his place as the pride male.

OPPOSITE PAGE, BOTTOM: Fang was also the main protector of the three youngest cubs.

joined in. The damp, still air created such ideal conditions that the sound of the roars could have been traveling seven or even eight kilometers. We were just twenty-five meters away, where the roars were so deafening that they actually took on a physical presence. So much so, it felt as if an iron band was being wrapped around our chests making us short of breath.

Such strong demonstrations of the group's solidarity succeeded in keeping the neighbors at bay, but inside the pride there was a small tragedy brewing. Imperceptibly, one of the tiniest cubs had been losing weight and we noticed it trailing behind, wobbling slightly with weakness. Finally, it caught up with its mother and two siblings. But the next morning, as the mother and her two healthy cubs got up and walked toward the rest of the pride, the sick cub staggered feebly in the other direction and disappeared all on its own into thick vegetation at the bottom of a gully. We never saw it again.

A few days later, some of the females were wandering nonchalantly up a slope to join Layla and her cub, and en route they startled a warthog that ran straight toward Layla. Layla was able to grab the pig, but all the females rushed in to feed and elbowed her aside. Once again, Layla got nothing to eat, though her cub was in the thick of the scrum. Then Fang arrived and tried to pull the carcass away while the females hung on, growling fearsomely. The ruckus they were making attracted unwelcome attention. Two intruders appeared on the skyline just one hundred meters from the pride. They were powerful males, and certainly more than equal in size to Fang.

In the mayhem of trying to eat, none of our lions noticed the approaching lions, who were the most deadly of adversaries. No strangers to us, they were part of the biggest coalition in the Mara; and the extraordinary history of the oldest lion in the group was well-known to all the driver guides in the reserve.

In 2005, he had been one half of a male pair that had dominated the Bila Shaka pride in the area close to where Sita had given birth. At this point, his nose had a distinctive slit so the driver guides called him Notch. Then, in the same year, his companion was killed, leaving him on his own. It wasn't long before he was driven from the Bila Shaka pride by a coalition of three males. However, he had a safety net provided by a group of younger male lions, some of whom might have been his sons. He was accepted into the group, and for a year or two the gang lived on its own. The young males grew big and powerful, and in August 2008, the old king was on the threshold of a new lease on life. As the years had passed, the distinctive slit in his nose had healed, and he needed a new name. Kali means "fierce" in Swahili, and we decided this was appropriate.

We never knew if there were seven or eight male lions in the group as they were never all together in one place. However many there were, though,

PAGES 60–61: From 6,000 meters up in the air, the sinuous loops of the Mara River can clearly be seen.

OPPOSITE PAGE: One of the youngest cubs suddenly looked weak and thin.

the group was about to take the Masai Mara by storm. We had no doubt that they would have a huge impact on all the lion prides nearby, and maybe touch Sita's life too.

Right now it was our lion pride that was in trouble, but at least it looked as though there were only two of the coalition on the attack. They came closer and closer, and we realized one of them was Kali himself. Both lions held themselves stiffly, their eyes narrowed to slits. We'd never seen lions look so aggressive. But still, none of our lions was aware that danger was approaching.

At the last minute, one of the females suddenly glanced up, but by then the aggressors were on top of them. Fang looked up and instead of defending the pride, he immediately ran away. This was the catalyst for pandemonium to break out. Only by watching the footage later could we see the exact sequence of events, and it was astonishing.

Out of all six of the females, it was Layla who ran forward, summoning up all her energy and flagging physical strength to attack Kali and his companion. She was less than half their weight and size, but her assault was so fierce and unexpected that both males were taken aback—though only for a few seconds. Quickly, they recovered their composure and violently lunged forward. Layla fled, but handicapped by her injury, she was overtaken. The males circled her and, in a flash, one lashed out with his front paw, striking her so hard that she tumbled, head over tail, coming to rest immobile on the ground. However, she'd succeeded in giving the other females time to run off and hide the cubs in the bushes—though we hadn't seen Layla's cub with them. Now the females rushed back and joined the fray. Their snarls, bites, and charges deflected the attention of the marauders away from Layla's inert body.

A member of Kali's gang. They looked magnificent to us but they were a deadly threat to our pride.

As we watched the confrontation, we were on tenterhooks expecting other males from Kali's coalition to appear as backup. Luckily none of them did, but even so the fight swung in the balance. Then Fang strode calmly and powerfully forward from where he had been observing. He was roaring and frothing at the mouth. He looked magnificent and the attackers beat a retreat.

As they vanished over the horizon, Fang began an hour-long patrol, urinating on bushes as a way of broadcasting his scent and roaring to reassert his authority. We followed him but soon returned to Layla. She lay motionless, and there was no sign of her cub. We carefully drove forward and found that she was still breathing. This time, however, it looked as if she'd been paralyzed.

We waited at a circumspect distance from her for hour after hour. But by the time we had to go back to camp for the night, she hadn't stirred and her cub hadn't appeared. As we drove away, we tried not to think that her cub had been killed or about what could happen to Layla in the dark hours to come.

ABOVE: After the confrontation, Fang grimaced as he smelled out the places where the intruding males had been.

OPPOSITE PAGE: Lionesses are much smaller and weaker than male lions but will stalwartly defend their cubs against intruding males.

Leaving the camp before sunrise, we never knew what the day had in store for Sita or if it would be any or all of the cubs' last, as it was not just the lion pride that seemed to be constantly close to danger. Sita and her cubs were living every day on the edge, but so far, her first few days away from the den had passed without major incident. Then, one morning, her luck ran out.

We found Sita perched atop a termite mound, with her cubs huddled up to her for warmth. Despite being just one hundred kilometers from the equator, the Mara is cold at night because of its high altitude, some 1,500 meters above sea level. Sita often rested on top of a mound, since this gave her the safety of a vantage point from which she could watch for food and enemies. This morning, her caution proved crucial. Heading toward her, she spotted a male lion with a lioness from the Bila Shaka pride. The lions had yet to see Sita and the cubs and so, watching from a distance, we expected Sita to just slink away with her cubs and hide. But clearly, we still had much to learn about Sita. What we saw next defined the skill, courage, and sheer determination that characterized this mother.

Rather than move off in fear, Sita sat on top of the mound, holding her ground until she was noticed by the lions. Once she was spotted, the male lion walked straight toward her with purpose. His eyes said it all. His stare was cold and penetrating, fixed on Sita. This wasn't an expression of stalking prey; this look meant that the lion was heading for a fight.

Sita was no match for the male lion, who was easily five times her size, but remarkably she continued to hold her ground. Then, to our horror and amazement, she hunched her back and began to stalk toward the lion, as though it were a feeble gazelle. Her cubs still lacked their mother's nerve and scattered off into the grass near her, too fearful to leave their mother and run away. The cubs had reason to be afraid. Lions are intolerant of other predators on their territory and are notorious for hunting down and killing cheetah cubs.

OPPOSITE PAGE and PAGES 70–71: Sita spent much of the day resting on the top of termite mounds. While her carefree cubs played with abandon, she would use the vantage point provided by the mound to watch for potential danger.

OPPOSITE PAGE: Lions are the Mara's most powerful predators, so Sita and her cubs were extremely wary of them. The size and strength of male lions make them terrifying beasts, but they lack agility, allowing Sita to easily outmaneuver them. Lionesses are the greater threat to cheetahs, since their agility is more of a match.

THIS PAGE: Young cubs have only one way to defend themselves against predators: hide. With the cover of the long grass, all they can do is wait as their mother attempts to lure an approaching animal away from them.

The male lion seemed somewhat taken aback by Sita's bravery. He paused, perhaps in disbelief, while she continued to come toward him. Then suddenly he had had enough. He charged toward her at full speed. Sita, again to our amazement, ran toward the lion, and then, at the very last second, turned and fled. Her strategy was becoming clear: she was luring the lion away from her cubs. Realizing the danger at last, her cubs began to run away in panic as the hopelessly outpaced lion chased Sita into the distance. But then the lioness, who had been with the male, entered the fray. She charged at Sita with more speed, force, and determination than her male counterpart. There was real danger that Sita could be trapped between the two lions. But she quickened her pace and managed to escape the pair. Thankfully, the lions did not spot Sita's fleeing cubs. Lacking the energy to match Sita's speed, the two lions gave up, wandering off to continue their patrol across their territory.

Sita had faced a life-or-death situation that morning, for both herself and her cubs. And she'd risen to the challenge, showing us her bitter determination and courage, drilled into her by years of experience as she lost cubs from previous litters. But this would be the first of many such challenges before her cubs reached adulthood. She had won one battle, but her cubs' fate remained far from certain. Following her during the coming months was going to run our nerves ragged. But if our cheetah family was going to test our nerves, we were going to get little relief from the lions.

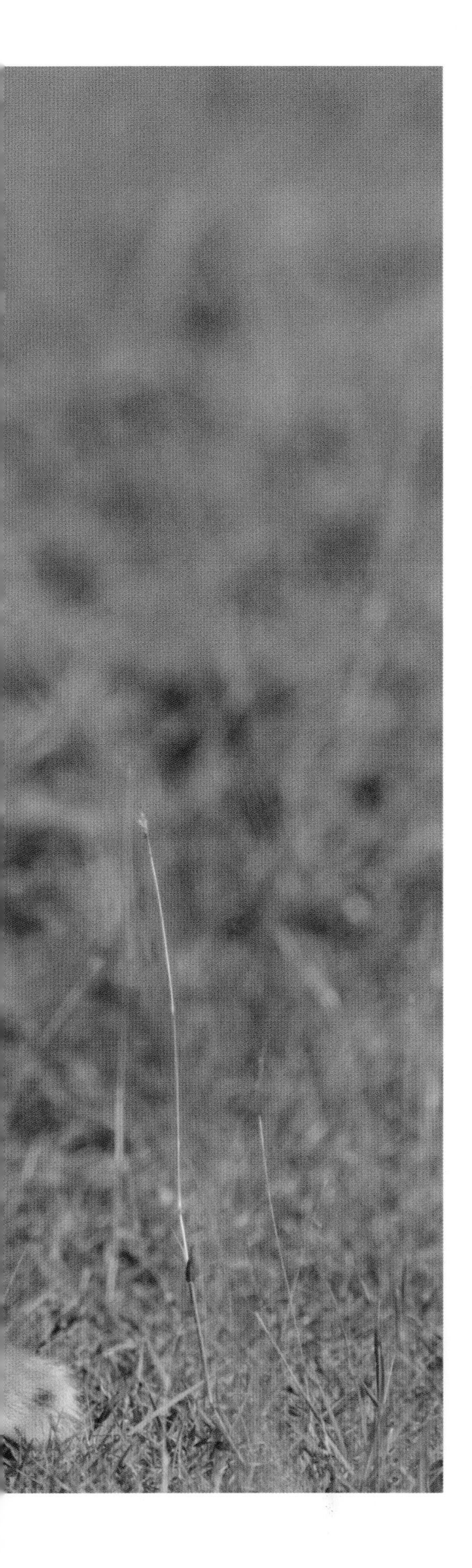

As we traveled in the early morning toward the spot where we'd left Layla after the fight, we were so worried about what we'd find that we hardly dared look. We were incredibly relieved to find her still alive. But then we saw that she hadn't moved nor had her cub turned up. Our spirits sank though the larks were in full voice, and a huge herd of impalas was browsing on the hills in the distance, their tails flickering like white flames in the low light.

As the sun rose higher, Layla raised her head, carefully, without moving her body. She called sadly and softly for her missing cub. Her calls increased in volume. But there was no answer, and slowly she laid her head back down again. The minutes crawled by as the heat began to intensify. Minutes became hours, and our thoughts turned to the day before. It was obvious from the quick thinking and speed with which she'd put herself on the front line that Layla's attack was a well-rehearsed event. She must have saved the pride like this many times before, so it was no wonder that her body carried so many scars and that she'd developed such a bad limp. After all that, it didn't seem fair that her cub had been killed; and if she really had been paralyzed, we couldn't help thinking that it was a pitiful end for such a fighter.

Suddenly there was a faint call behind us. Layla lifted her head. There was another call, closer still. With great effort, Layla got herself up into a sitting position. We searched the bushes using our binoculars but couldn't see anything apart from leaves and grasses.

Another low call came and we saw the cub running toward her mother. Layla lowered her head and the cub rubbed herself against her mother's face, time and time again. Their pleasure was plain to see, and our spirits soared, especially when Layla hauled herself to her feet. She groaned, her upper lip curled in pain, and she panted heavily with the effort. But at least she could move.

The mother and daughter had completely won our hearts and minds. During the next few weeks, it was a profoundly unsettling and humbling experience to watch Layla battle day after day, both to survive and to provide for her cub. Since the cub now seemed to embody the wild, unquenchable spirit of the place, we called her Mara.

Layla's spirited defense of the pride and her cub had won our hearts and minds.

Similarly, Sita's willingness to put her life on the line for her cubs' protection was equally humbling to witness. However, her apparent courage was about to be severely tested once again. Although she did not realize it, Sita was also being tracked by a gang of three powerful male cheetah brothers. We had followed the brothers since they were almost as young as Sita's cubs, when working on *Big Cat Diary*, and their growth to adulthood was quite a story.

Despite being similar in appearance, male and female cheetahs have very different lifestyles. Females, when they are not raising cubs, are solitary animals. They roam over vast areas called "home ranges," some several hundred square kilometers, and they do not fight to hold a territory. They roam these spaces to seek out gazelles as the herds migrate. But even the Mara, despite being one of the richest grasslands in the world, can only support a handful of cheetahs. Scientists estimate that one adult cheetah needs an area, on average, equivalent to more than thirteen times the size of Manhattan, to provide enough food for their survival.

While some male cheetahs roam as far as females, most male cheetahs will try to take and retain a much smaller territory. Then they become very territorial, scent-marking their patch of land and fighting any male that dares intrude. Male battles for territory are vicious; often the loser will be killed. When holding territory, there is safety in numbers so males are rarely solitary, instead teaming up to form a coalition. These gangs of males are usually, though not exclusively, made up of brothers who stick together from birth. Holding territory comes with rewards, as the males get to mate with any "in-season" female who wanders onto their patch.

Male and female cheetahs are so different that they even hunt different prey. The females specialize in hunting small gazelles, especially the Thomson's variety. The smaller, agile female cheetahs can cope with the high-speed maneuvers of these diminutive antelope. The bigger male cheetahs, often in their coalitions, rarely hunt small gazelles. Instead they target larger animals like zebra foals and even adult wildebeests and topi; animals that are so large they are usually only hunted by lions.

With all their powers, the three brothers had managed to carve out the Rhino Ridge area of the Masai Mara for themselves. Sita gave birth on the edge of their patch and regulary had to cross over Rhino Ridge to find the gazelle herds. She was on a collision course, and at some stage they were bound to meet. This was a worrisome prospect, as we were aware that male cheetahs sometimes harmed small cubs the age of Sita's offspring.

PAGE 76: As Sita trekked across the plains, she frequently crossed the territory of three cheetah brothers. Whereas female cheetahs roam the plains solitarily, males have a tendency to form fiercely territorial coalitions.

PAGES 78–79: The cheetah brothers scent-marked trees and bushes across their territory to proclaim their boundary to other cheetahs in the area.

ABOVE: The cheetah brothers spent their days patrolling their territory, to ensure that rival males did not stray onto their patch. But crucially for Sita, they were also on the lookout for females with whom they could potentially mate.

OPPOSITE PAGE: The cheetah brothers were an inseparable team, constantly showing affection to one another.

We first met the cheetah brothers as small cubs in 2006 filming their mother, Honey, rearing them through the first years of their lives. Then, in February 2007, tragedy struck. One of the cubs had been slightly injured climbing a tree, having been chased by baboons. Honey also had a superficial injury. A wildlife vet arrived on the scene and decided to treat the injuries. There is fierce debate about whether it is morally right to intervene to help a sick or injured wild animal—especially if it is threatened, as are cheetahs—or leave well alone and let nature take its course. In this instance, the vet responsible decided to dart the injured cheetahs, to sedate them for treatment. Anesthetizing any animal always carries a risk. Honey was unlucky, and some part of the procedure resulted in her death and her cubs being orphaned. It was a tragedy, and memories of her loss still upset those of us who knew this courageous and confident cheetah so well.

The cubs were still too young to hunt for themselves. If the authorities had left them to their own devices, they probably would have starved to death. The park rangers decided to feed the cubs regularly. Over time, the rangers made their meals less frequent, to encourage the cubs to hunt for themselves. It worked, and the orphans survived to adulthood to become the cheetah lords of Rhino Ridge. Watching the brothers now, strong, healthy, and in their prime, is all the more impressive knowing their history. But our compassion for the boys was about to be tested.

Sita's five cubs were now ten weeks old, having survived a month away from the den. It had been a nerve-racking time, with distant lions and hyenas patrolling around Sita's patch, but Sita's experience had so far kept her cubs safe. We followed Sita constantly during the day, but at dusk we had to leave her and head back to camp. At night, anything could happen to Sita. So every evening, as the red sun sank behind the Mara escarpment, we left feeling anxious for Sita and her cubs. All we could do was hope that the cubs would be alive and well the next morning. Night is dangerous in the Mara; this is when the carnivores come alive. Dozy lions during the day suddenly gain a dangerous sparkle in their eyes and stride across the plains with domineering confidence.

Spotted hyenas appear everywhere, emerging from their dens and hollows. They are the most abundant predator on the plains, and the most misunderstood. Many dismiss them as scavengers rather than recognizing them for what they are: supreme predators. Hyenas run down most of their meals, hunting alone or in packs; either way, they are ruthlessly efficient. In fact, it is often the lions that come to scavenge off hyena kills, and not the other way around. Hyenas are often portrayed as "the bad guys" when, in reality, they are just another predator struggling to survive and raise their young.

One stormy evening, Sita made a kill. We had to return to camp, but this was worrisome to us, coming at a time when the hyenas and other predators would be rising from their slumbers. As darkness fell, her enemies had yet to spot her, but the family was still close to the carcass. For a moment, Sita's cautious nature seemed to have slipped. The next morning, we found her at dawn. Something was wrong. She was on a termite mound, calling and calling, her plaintive bird-like cry piercing the misty air. Only three cubs were huddled by her side. They clung to her nervously as she called. Sita eventually left the mound and started to search the area, sniffing in the grass, still calling and calling. She was clearly looking for her lost cubs and continually returned to one clump of grass. A tiny spot of blood was all that marked where a tragedy might have occurred. We still hoped that a little lost cub would suddenly come bounding out of the grass to her mother, but it never happened. Like before, we never saw those two cubs again.

There are more hyenas on the African plains than any other predator. They survive either by scavenging on carcasses caught by cats or by catching their own prey.

Sita finally gave up her painstaking search and started to walk away from the area. Whoever had killed her cubs, be they lions or hyenas, might still be nearby, so she did not want to endanger the surviving cubs. Unfortunately, the direction of her march was taking her toward even more trouble.

High on the ridge above her, we noticed the cheetah brothers. They were sitting in a croton thicket, watching Sita and her cubs intently. Sita had failed to spot them. We were concerned because the relationship between male and female cheetahs is far from romantic. The territorial males were likely to chase down Sita and brutally take her captive to see if she was in season to mate. Sita was still suckling her cubs and far from being ready to mate, but the brothers might still take her to make sure. The big worry was what would happen to the cubs. Invading male lions nearly always kill lion cubs, to bring the lionesses into season so that they can father their own. Since cheetah males do not have a pride of females, the females they mate with come and go, and thus the male cheetahs are never sure of the paternity of the cubs. So unlike lions, they generally do not kill cubs. But some do, so any encounter was uncertain. As Sita approached the brothers, we feared that her already terrible day was about to get even worse.

Sita walked closer and closer to the brothers, with her three remaining cubs in tow. The cheetah males watched her as though she was an approaching gazelle, hunched and ready to strike. Finally, they burst out of the bushes, charging straight at Sita. She had no time to escape and was bowled over by the larger males. The cubs scattered into the grass and disappeared. The boys' attention was fixated on Sita, forcing her onto her back, as she tried to

OPPOSITE PAGE, TOP: As the sun set, the fall of darkness brought with it even greater danger for Sita's cubs. Every night, there was a real possibility that the cubs would not survive to the morning.

OPPOSITE PAGE, BOTTOM: One night, the nightmare became a reality. At daybreak, Sita was surrounded by only three cubs. The missing two were never seen again.

ABOVE: When the cheetah brothers spotted Sita within their territory, they went on the offensive, hunting her down as a potential mate.

OPPOSITE PAGE: While it may appear that the males treat the female with extreme brutality, rarely does the behavior result in any injury to either side.

PAGES 88–89: Our last view of the reserve after four months of filming. While we were away, our thoughts were never far from either the cheetahs or lions.

fend them off with her paws and claws. But with three attackers, they were bound to get the better of her as they tried to sniff the base of her tail and find out if she was in season. It was difficult to watch. The brothers were so brutal, aggressively growling as they repeatedly attacked Sita who was constantly calling out in defense or submission.

After a few hours, the brothers tired of harassing Sita and retired to a nearby termite mound. Sita's cubs were huddled together in the grass, just fifty meters away. Then the inevitable happened. One of the brothers spotted the cubs. He slunk off the termite mound and began to stalk them, just like he would with prey. The two other brothers instantly recognized the hunting position, and joined him on each side. Shoulder to shoulder, they stalked in synchrony toward the terrified cubs. Then they broke into a charge, running straight at the little huddle. At the last second, two of the cubs ran for their lives. But one held its ground, screaming at its attackers before scuttling off to find her two siblings.

Mercifully, the brothers had stopped their attack at the very last second. They still hounded the little creatures, hunching up their shoulders to look even bigger and more threatening. They growled at the frightened cubs but thankfully they never touched them. Meanwhile, Sita called frantically for her cubs. After what seemed like a lifetime, they heard her calls and scurried back to their mother. It was a huge relief when the bullying brothers finally walked away.

Witnessing this event, it would have been easy to take sides. However, often one's emotions and judgments get clouded as dramas like these unfold. What we had seen was simply what cheetahs do, and it is part of a lifestyle that has evolved to make them the supreme cats that they are. We are disturbed by the often savage and apparently unjust events of the natural world and feel a need to bring order to it. However, it is this "wildness" that creates its magnificence and beauty, and this always surpasses its darker side. It is impossible to try to tame or order nature without running the risk of destroying everything that it is.

Five weeks after the males attacked Sita, and after Layla had valiantly defended the pride and saved her cub, we faced a dilemma. The filming equipment needed servicing and cleaning; should we stay or should we go? In the end, we returned to our offices in England, but during our month away, neither cheetahs nor lions were ever far from our thoughts.

PART TWO

We returned to the Masai Mara in late January 2009 to the surprise discovery that in our absence, the lion pride crossed the Mara River in search of food. Yet again to our surprise, on the very first day we caught up with them, we found everyone together—even Layla and Mara. Not only that, but Layla was walking far better than we'd ever seen.

In the next few weeks, the lions kept us on our toes by crossing the river twice more. As a result of this predilection for going back and forth, we decided to call our lions the River Pride. Unfortunately we never saw them crossing. We wondered if they chose to go at night and whether it was easier for them to avoid crocodiles this way. It's so rare for lions to go swimming or wading that we couldn't help but hope to see it one day. Most of the riverbank was hidden from us by thick vegetation and impossible to access, so the chances of seeing the event were slim indeed.

The zebras and wildebeests had long gone in search of fresh grasses to the north and south of the reserve, but larger animals like buffalo and eland still roamed the thickets and grasslands. However, both seemed too imposing and dangerous for the River Pride to tackle. There were also smaller antelope such as topi as well as several species of gazelles, but all these seemed to be too vigilant and swift. Sometimes, we found one or two of the pride early in the morning chewing thoughtfully on the remains of an impala or a Thomson's gazelle, so it seemed that occasionally they were able to ambush one at night. Generally, they concentrated on hunting warthogs. Since warthogs are active in the day, that meant the lions were busy too. Statistics show that lions can be inactive, or conserving their energy, for an average of twenty-three out of every twenty-four hours, so we relished the opportunity to witness any daytime activity, though we couldn't help feeling it was at the lions' expense.

Hunting warthogs isn't easy. The pigs are small short-legged animals; the grasses were long, and after days and days of being stalked and chased by lions, the surviving warthogs were extraordinarily alert to the slightest noise or movement. We couldn't move because the moment they heard our cars' engines start up, every pig in the neighborhood would lift its head, sniff, and rush off. We had to be careful not to ruin the pride's chances, for there were eighteen lions existing on meager scraps and every hunt was vital and hard.

Stalking through the dry grasses was almost impossible for the lions without being heard or spotted by the pigs themselves or by topi and giraffes. If the pigs heard a topi's alarm snort or saw a giraffe staring, they would run off immediately without a second thought.

Even if the lions were able to creep close enough to risk the loss of energy on a high-speed chase, the pigs usually outran them, darting and weaving between the hungry cats. When a pig was eventually caught, every lion would rush to snatch a piece of meat. There would be no sign of a carcass, just a heaving mass of hungry lions, young and old, fighting to get a share.

If Mara was lucky to be with the pride, she was the most desperate of all the lions to feed. Layla's limp had become much worse once again, and we wondered if she'd fallen off the rocks while crossing the river. Our optimism at Layla's improvement at the beginning of the trip had slipped away, and we noticed that Layla was now with the pride so rarely that both she and her cub were painfully thin.

When the two of them *were* with the pride, they seemed to gravitate toward the female with the two small cubs, though she rebuffed their friendly overtures with a menacing growl. Despite this, Layla seemed intent on creating a special relationship with her. We called the other female, Malaika, the Swahili word for "angel," and it proved to be particularly apt.

One afternoon, a tremendous storm rolled in. As the dark clouds thickened and the wind howled, the lions crouched, their ears flat, waiting for the inevitable rain. When the cold downpour began, some moved into the vegetation; others, pragmatically, huddled in the open. Just before dark, the rain dwindled and stopped, and as the lions gathered, happy to be together again, Layla made straight for Malaika. For once, Malaika let her lick her face and ears; she even reciprocated. It was the first and only time we ever saw any of the pride respond to Layla's overtures.

PAGE 93: We had seen that the Mara River is a formidable obstacle to cross for wildebeests and zebras so we were amazed to find that the pride crossed it too.

OPPOSITE PAGE, TOP: Warthogs are very difficult for lions to hunt.

OPPOSITE PAGE, BOTTOM: Food was so scarce that each member of the pride struggled to get a share of the kill.

ABOVE: Layla and Mara were so rarely with the pride and feeding so infrequently that they were getting very thin.

The next morning, we saw Mara playing, walking, and feeding with Malaika's cubs, and as the day continued, it seemed as if she'd been "adopted" or "handed over" to Malaika. But whatever the relationship was, it wasn't an easy transition.

Malaika was never particularly friendly to the newcomer and often growled as she got near, but at least she tolerated the youngster's presence. In the first few days, as Mara moved off with Malaika and the pride, the cub would often linger, looking wistfully back for some sign of her mother. Maybe she was torn between the choice of following the pride or sticking with her mother, but slowly her hesitation disappeared, and after that she never looked back. Lions are social animals and it seemed to us that from that point on, Mara became more settled and less anxious. She would often initiate play with the two youngest cubs. We wondered if this was from sheer, simple enjoyment or whether it was a chance for her to forge bonds with them in preparation for the future or maybe it strengthened her bond with her "stepmother." Perhaps it was a mixture of all three.

Mara's future with Malaika and the pride might well have been brighter for her than staying with her mother, but we couldn't imagine what it was like for Layla to lose her cub. After all the years Layla had spent defending the pride, fate had dealt her a truly bitter blow.

On March 12, we found Layla resting on the edge of the pride. Her tummy was full, and she was even walking well. Though Mara seemed unaware of her, playing with the cubs and keeping close to Malaika, we thought maybe Layla's fortunes had finally improved. Just then, we got a big surprise, for

ABOVE: Mara with her "stepmother" Malaika and one of Malaika's small cubs.

OPPOSITE PAGE, TOP: Layla set off, unhesitatingly, on her own, leaving Mara and the pride behind.

OPPOSITE PAGE, BOTTOM: At first, Mara, when she was with the pride, would often look back to see if Layla was following.

Layla got up and unhesitatingly set off to the north without looking back. We followed her as she passed groups of waterbuck and buffalo and soon, she'd left the pride well behind. She even tried to stalk a warthog, though it seemed more of a brief burst of optimism than a well-thought-out hunt with purpose.

Her adventure continued as she came across a lone lioness and her cubs resting in a clump of long grasses. It was Luna, the female with three cubs that we'd noticed living on the margin of the pride back in the early days. Since Luna looked so similar to Layla, we'd assumed she was probably a daughter from one of Layla's previous litters and ostracized for some unknown reason from the pride.

There was a tentative but warm greeting between them all, and then Layla set off again still heading north. After three more kilometers, she was limping badly once again and lay down to rest in the shade of a small bush. We couldn't imagine why she'd left Mara and the pride in such a determined fashion.

ABOVE and OPPOSITE PAGE: Our last sights of Layla; we never saw her alive again.

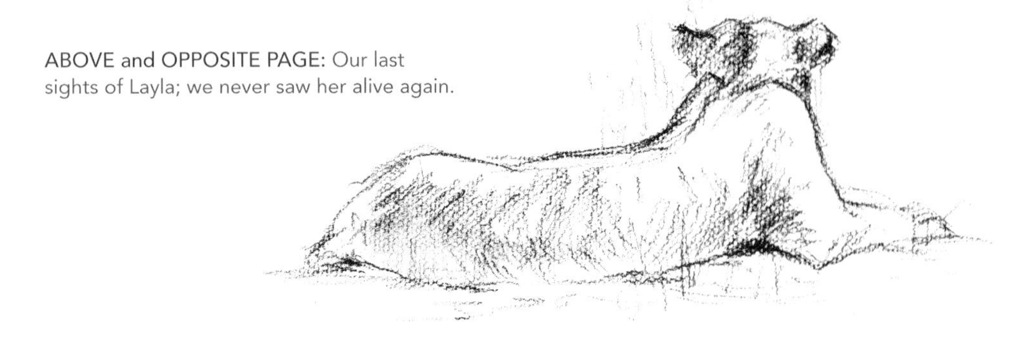

We spent the rest of the afternoon watching Layla sleep peacefully in the shade of a small bush before we traveled fifteen kilometers or so back to our camp for the night. We searched the area for her the next day and the next but never saw her again. And in due course, we could only surmise that she'd died. We have known one lioness in the wild to have lived for nineteen years, but the average lifespan is much shorter. However old Layla was, we had one simple hope that after all her struggles, her heart had simply given up so she'd been able to die peacefully.

With the death of her mother, Mara became the focus of our hopes—and fears. We wanted to see her live both for her own sake and to keep her mother's memory alive. But she was still not even a year old; she needed another year or eighteen months of stability in which to grow up. That was a long time indeed, and not much of it had passed before we were reminded just how vulnerable Fang, and therefore the pride, was.

One morning, as the pride was waking up, we saw a strange male just a half-kilometer away on the other side of a shallow gully. As one or two lionesses spotted him, he slowly got to his feet and narrowed his eyes before walking forward, slowly and stiff-legged. It was exactly the same behavior we'd seen earlier when Kali had attacked, but at least this time around, the pride had spotted him before he was too close. Fang stood up to watch as the intruder came closer and closer. He stayed still until the last moment and when he turned to run, one of the older lionesses moved forward to intercept the stranger in exactly the same way that Layla had done before.

She half-crouched in front of the stranger to draw his attention away from the other females who ran off with the cubs and youngsters. We saw Mara tuck herself in the middle of the fleeing group while, a kilometer away, Fang peeped over the horizon to see what would happen next.

The strange male, rigid with tension, approached the lioness. She glanced back at the pride still on the run in the distance, and then at the male. Almost moving sideways, he moved closer and closer. She held herself steady until, at the very last minute, she snarled and slashed out at him with needle-sharp claws extended. Undeterred, he continued to move forward, and she crouched in front of him again in a half-submissive and half-aggressive position. He was almost touching her when there was an explosive movement and an outbreak of noise. The other females had crept back and were on the attack. In defense, he turned on the females, lashing out with his paws and lunging forward. He tried to slash them with his teeth until at last they let him go.

As he ran off, limping slightly, blood trickled down his body from numerous small gashes and cuts. They'd bitten him on his rump and raked his body and face with their claws. Our hands shook for several minutes afterward.

At times, the lions had come so close to us that we'd been just a mere ten meters away from the action. During the past few months while we'd been watching the lions rest, sleep, and walk, it had been easy to forget just how intimidating, even frightening, they could be. However, despite the power and fury, neither the females nor the male had hurt each other as much as they could have. It had been more a display of bravado and bluff than a life-threatening battle.

Meanwhile, as soon as the females had caught their breath, they regrouped with the cubs and youngsters and led them, without stopping, on a journey to safety through bushes and gullies for some three kilometers or more. For the rest of the day, they relaxed in the shade of the bushes. It was then that we recognized the female who had stepped into Layla's shoes. We'd nicknamed her "Grumpy Gran" sometime before because she had never been anything but irritable with the youngsters and cubs. Now she'd laid her life on the line in order to save them all.

Disturbingly, Fang didn't reappear and we hoped he hadn't gone for good. Not only did Mara and the other cubs need him, we'd grown fond of him. He was an idiosyncratic lion with what seemed to be a particularly eccentric outlook on Malaika's tiny cubs. Though they were desperate to greet him whenever he appeared, he'd usually be quite flummoxed and taken aback by their advances and would often trot away from them looking quite alarmed.

Now that we'd seen him run away twice from two major confrontations, it would have been easy for us to label him a coward. But we reminded ourselves that he had lost his male companions months before, as well as one of his dagger-like canine teeth, so we saw him more as a fallen hero. The big question now was "Would he come back?" Concern for Mara and the pride was uppermost in our minds since they seemed to be more at risk than ever before.

PAGES 101–103 and OPPOSITE PAGE: After the confrontation, the pride traveled for some three kilometers before they felt safe enough to settle and lick each other for reassurance, at which point we were particularly pleased to see Mara being comforted by her "stepmother."

In a typical year, the Masai Mara is blessed by rain during most months. The Mara is close to Lake Victoria, which is such a vast inland sea that it generates its own local weather. Storms created by the lake drift over the Mara escarpment and then release rain on the plains. This makes it one of the most productive grasslands for animals in the world. When the seasonal rains begin in November, the storms can become so heavy that you can easily forget it is a blessing. By midday, huge thunderclouds grow, and these merge into walls of blackness that relentlessly march across the plains. As the rain approaches, the wind arrives, sometimes strong enough to pick up a double tent with bed and furniture and toss it into the Mara River. Lightning flashes all around and when the rain hits, it's so heavy that you can barely see fifteen meters around you. Often hailstones fall, accompanied by deafening thunder. It is hardly the picturesque scene one imagines of the dry plains basking under a hot African sun.

From November to March, our cheetah family had to weather these daily storms. The rain would literally soak them to the skin, with Sita and her cubs looking as if they had just been fished out of the Mara River. The cubs were often reduced to shivering, and we feared that they could fall victim to exposure, a killer of many small cheetah cubs. But somehow they always seemed to bounce back.

Sita had wandered onto an area of the Masai Mara with fewer lions, probably due to the nature of the terrain and the bushy vegetation, but home to two very large hyena clans. One morning, Sita and the cubs encountered a couple of clan members. Hyenas always approach a cheetah to try their luck and see if they have just caught dinner. For an adult cheetah, this is just an irritation, but for a mother with cubs, it can be very dangerous. Hyenas, like most big African predators, kill any other predators' youngsters as they view them as competition as well as food. So Sita had to take these two advancing hyenas seriously.

The Masai Mara is one of the wettest grasslands in East Africa. The abundance of rain makes the land a haven for a remarkably high density of wildlife.

We were not surprised by Sita's response when she went straight onto the offensive. She stalked directly toward the hyena pair, but this time—unlike with the lions—she actually attacked, leaping over the second hyena and raking it with her claws. Both hyenas first backed off, looking disconcerted. But they soon came back at her and the commotion began to draw other hyenas onto the scene. Sita was fast becoming outnumbered.

The cubs had learned to retreat when their mother went into battle. Their problem this time was where to retreat to. Hyenas were appearing all over the place, pumped up with adrenaline, their tails waving in the air. They were ready for a fight. The situation was rapidly looking disastrous for the cheetah family. As the hyenas harried Sita and sniffed the grass to hunt out the cubs, the cubs darted from tussock to tussock trying to find somewhere to hide. The cubs were visibly shaking with fear.

But Sita's aggressive charges started to make a difference. The hyenas realized Sita wouldn't be quick to back down so they began to drift away, looking for an easier opportunity for a meal. Eventually, the whole clan turned their attention away from Sita and her cubs. This time our cheetah family was lucky.

OPPOSITE PAGE: Hyenas roam the plains in clans that sometimes consist of more than a dozen members.

ABOVE: Despite their reputation as scavengers, hyenas are in fact ruthlessly efficient predators, hunting in packs and catching much of their own prey.

Though we couldn't describe the River Pride as being lucky, its members were keeping their heads above water. A few days after the confrontation with the intruders, we were pleased to find Fang back with the pride and very relieved that he hadn't abandoned them. The lionesses, though, still faced an uphill struggle to catch enough food for everyone in the pride. Then we found the group on the edge of the riverbank staring in fascination at the river, rushing by with floodwater. They started walking upstream. Grumpy Gran led in front, and Mara and the others walked behind. Every now and then, the whole group stopped to gaze warily at the raging torrent. We wondered why they wanted to cross the river when it was in full spate but realized that Grumpy Gran might be keen to boost their chances of success with fresh hunting grounds.

Sometimes they disappeared into the thick growth that crowded up to the water's edge, and we'd wait nervously on the other side of the bushes hoping that they hadn't tried to swim across, out of our sight. However, they kept on going, walking upstream, resting and walking again until an afternoon storm came rolling in. It was right then, as the thunder rumbled and the rain poured down, that Grumpy Gran paused, turned, and waded into the river, chest deep.

Spray from the frothing white rapids filled the air, muddy water whirled and crashed over the rocks, and the rain continued to pour down. It was a foreboding and potentially deadly scene.

Grumpy Gran stopped and hissed at the water. We were appalled at the strength of the current and convinced that she shouldn't attempt to cross. While she hesitated, the others huddled behind her, so close to each other that the pride itself took on a strange, amorphous shape that flowed and eddied as different lions moved around within the group. Suddenly, Grumpy Gran was pushed from behind. She lost her footing and slipped deeper into the water almost unable to regain control.

We could hardly bear to watch; fresh in our minds was a horrific story we'd been told about the same females swimming the river when it was filled high with floodwater two years earlier. They had eleven small cubs with them at the time, and people on safari watched helplessly as nine of these were swept away in the torrent and drowned in the rapid tumble of the water further downstream.

When Grumpy Gran turned around and the group, still acting as a whole, scrambled up the bank and away, we were greatly relieved. The next day, they were on the move again. They headed downstream, close to the river,

retracing their steps from the day before. However, they'd only gone a few hundred meters when they popped down a gully close to the water and disappeared. We waited on the other side, but none of them came back out. The river was still high and we could see all the way across to the other side, but there wasn't a lion to be seen. We maneuvered to get a better view and were totally surprised at the sight that greeted us on the edge of the water.

The pride had found a dead hippo partly washed up on the shore and were clustered around its body. After weeks of eating so little, they finally had a marvelous chance for a feast.

But they were not alone. Crocodiles, attracted by the smell of blood, were already gathering in the water just behind the dead hippo. The lions glanced around nervously. More crocodiles arrived and one female lost her patience. She rushed at the water, snarling ferociously and trying to chase the closest crocodile away. Instead, it stayed, gold-green eyes unblinkingly fixed on the carcass while others took heart and moved even closer. Suddenly, Fang noticed the threat, pounded into the water, and splashed out to the crocodile. They glared balefully at each other, eye to eye, before Fang struck out at the crocodile so violently that it backed away a little. Fang followed up his advantage, roaring again and again until the crocodile swam off followed by the rest. In all our years filming lions, we had never seen such an encounter, and Fang, we thought, acquitted himself very well.

The next day, the lions were so full of food that even though the morning wasn't warm, they were panting heavily. Hot and heavy with meat, they could hardly move, though a few, including Mara, were still gamely feeding on the stinking remains, their swollen tummies swinging like barrage balloons. The day after, Fang had dragged the remains of the carcass up onto the bank and well out of the crocodiles' reaches. His actions in defending the lucky find had proved how valuable he was to the pride. None of the crocodiles got a mouthful of hippo. All the lions had benefited, and there was no pride that deserved a better break.

PAGE 111: Hunger was driving the pride's need to cross the river, but the waters were far too high for comfort.

PAGES 112–113: Understandably, the pride was cautious about approaching the river with its hungry crocodiles on the prowl so they left Fang on his own to pull the heavy carcass away from the dangerous waters.

OPPOSITE PAGE: It was up to Fang to protect the carcass from marauding crocodiles; if one reptile had started to eat, dozens would follow.

Time passed and we'd now been following our cheetah family for five months. Sita's three remaining cubs had grown in stature and confidence. We could clearly see that the cubs were all females, and so if they were to survive to independence, they would be a wonderful addition to the breeding population of the Masai Mara and northern Serengeti area. Since their ordeal with the hyenas, the cubs had become far faster on their feet—little cheetahs that could dodge and outrun their enemies. They had also learned another vital trick: tree climbing. This was especially effective with hyenas who, like dogs, have absolutely no skills in this department. As soon as a harassing hyena appeared, the cubs would shoot up the nearest tree and watch it pass from a safe height. This seemed to take pressure off Sita too, who no longer felt the need to attack the hyenas to draw them away from the cubs. She now seemed almost nonchalant whenever her old enemies appeared. There was just one snag. The cubs often found it easier to scale a tree than to come down, and many a time they sat nervously, staring at the perilous drop below, trying to summon up the courage to leap down.

On one particular day, it became clear that things had really changed. Sita had run down a male Thomson's gazelle, and all the family were feeding on it. But a large male lion was advancing through the bushes toward them and their kill, and the cheetah family seemed totally unaware of the danger. When Sita finally looked up and saw him coming, she instantly growled a warning. Her cubs scattered from the carcass, but surprisingly not very far. Sita then went into her now-familiar attack posture and started to stalk straight toward the giant beast. He was bemused by the audacity and crouched down into an ambush position, ready to pounce, his tail lashing in fury.

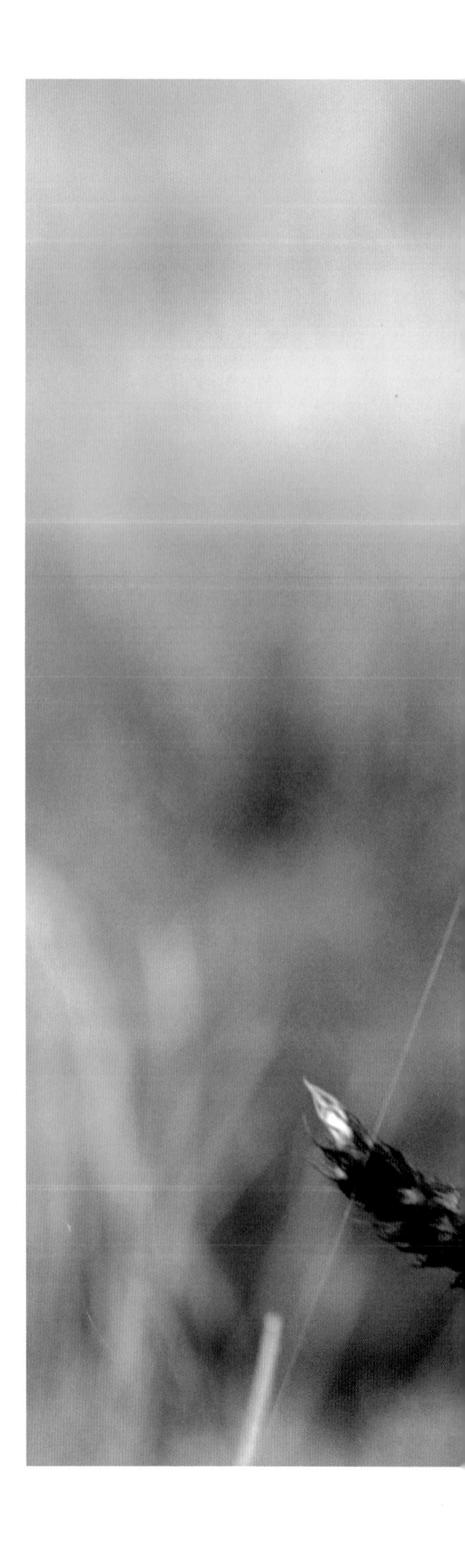

The cubs had learned new skills such as tree climbing. They seemed to find this great fun, but more importantly, it allowed them to escape from hyenas.

THIS PAGE and OPPOSITE PAGE: Sita and her cubs found that hyenas were no longer the nightmare that they had been. When a hyena was nearby, the cheetahs would watch it intently but firmly hold their ground. Sita seemed almost nonchalant surrounded by her old enemies.

Sita kept on coming directly at him. With only a few yards separating the two cats, the lion finally had enough and leapt forward into a charge. Sita, being Sita, charged at him too, arching her body to try and appear a little bigger. She rushed right up to the fearsome lion who was also coming at her at full speed. At the very last moment, Sita turned and the lion ran after her and away from both the kill and the cubs. This was the closest Sita had been to a lion. He gave chase for a while, but big heavy male lions do not enjoy running about in the heat of the day, and this one soon gave up. Sita kept close to him, hassling him as he wandered off.

A male lion is so powerful that it can terrify and scatter a whole clan of a dozen or more hyenas, and yet Sita was treating this one with utter contempt. How times had changed. A month ago, she would have abandoned her meal and whisked the cubs away to safety. Not this time. She boldly strolled back to the dead gazelle and called to the cubs to join her. Cautiously, the cubs returned, and the whole family finished the meal with the male lion just one hundred meters away in the bushes.

It was the middle of April and time to go back to England again. Heavy rain was still falling, and after three and one-half months of stormy weather, it was becoming increasingly difficult to drive around. It was hard to leave both of our cat families, though we felt somewhat reassured because they both seemed to be doing so well. We should have known better.

PART THREE

The bad news filtered through to us only a day or two after we left. A blogger on the Mara Conservancy website wrote that a driver had found a dead lion near the riverbank not far from Headquarters One. No one knew who the lion was, but since this was the heart of the River Pride's home range, we felt sure it must be one of them. When we returned in early June, we found that there had indeed been a disaster.

The pride was in disarray. One of Malaika's cubs had a badly injured eye that it could hardly open. Malaika's "stepdaughter" Mara kept close to the injured cub but its sibling was missing as was one of the eight youngsters. Fang, Grumpy Gran, and another adult lioness weren't to be seen either. We guessed Kali and his gang had struck once again and this time had succeeded in getting rid of Fang. Over the next few days, we watched sadly as the survivors of the River Pride wandered around aimlessly.

Weeks later, a ranger claimed to have seen Fang heading across the border into Tanzania. It would be wonderful to think he was still alive somewhere and doing well, but we shall never know for sure.

Soon the remnants of the River Pride took to their heels to avoid Kali and his gang. We discovered how hard it was to find a pride on the run. The long grasses, taller than the adult females, exacerbated the difficulty. Sitting or standing, the whole pride could be completely hidden even though they were just a few meters away from our car. We caught glimpses of them every now and then until a fortnight later, when we managed to get a clear view of Malaika and her injured cub sitting high up on a termite mound in the warm rays of the afternoon sun. They were all alone.

Over the next few days, we were able to find them every day, since the little cub couldn't move far. Helplessly, we watched it struggle through the thick tangle of tall grasses, getting weaker and weaker, trying to keep up with Malaika. And though the cub hadn't seen its sibling for weeks, it would sometimes still sit up and call forlornly, a high and plaintive sound that tugged at our heartstrings. Poignantly, Malaika, who had never been a very attentive mother to any of her cubs, was now paying this little one particular attention. But it was too late. The cub became more and more listless until one day both Malaika and her cub were nowhere to be found.

We crossed the river to try and find the rest of the pride. Amazingly, we spotted them quickly and for the first time in weeks, we were able to see that Mara, who was with them, was still alive and well. To our surprise, Malaika was already there, greeting her adult companions like the long-lost friends they were. But her injured cub wasn't there, and we knew it had finally given

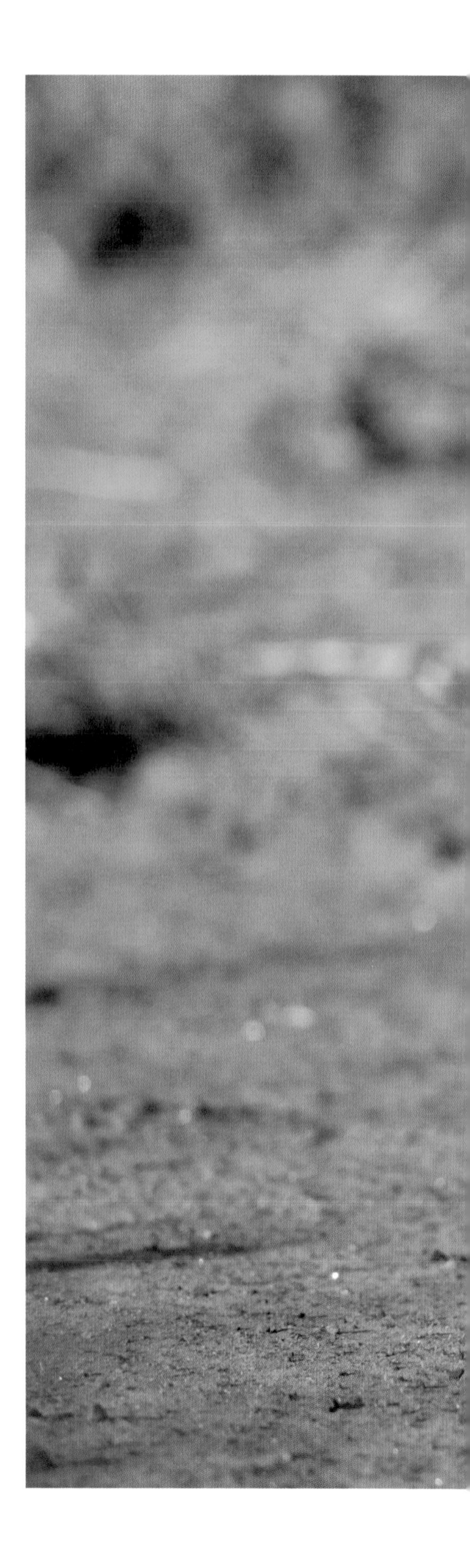

PAGE 123: Malaika had lost another of her own cubs; and, sadly, the remaining cub was badly injured.

TOP: It was a relief to see that Mara was still alive.

BOTTOM: Mara kept even closer to her "stepmother" than before.

OPPOSITE PAGE: The surviving members of the pride seemed unsure where they should go or what they should do.

up the struggle to live. With no tiny cubs left in the pride, we wondered if Malaika and her two adult female companions might accept the advances of Kali and his gang. That would mean Mara and the seven remaining youngsters would be left to their own devices and none of them had any experience in looking after themselves. Six months younger than the rest, Mara had been the unluckiest of them all; her mother had died and now the protection and help of her "stepmother" and aunts might be swept away too.

Just as the members of the River Pride seemed to be facing their darkest hour, we lost them totally. We guessed that they were hiding from Kali and

his gang, but as the days flew past, we began to think that something awful had happened to them. We redoubled our efforts and widened our searches by employing local safari guides to help.

One evening, off in the distance, we heard a muffled roar that sounded like surf breaking on a beach. The next day, the plains were full of animals. It was early July. The wildebeest herds had returned from Tanzania, and the plains were full of life once again. If the River Pride was okay, the arrival of the herds meant hunting had just become much easier for them.

Within a couple of days, the wildebeest herds split up and some crossed the river in search of fresh pastures in the south of the reserve. The waters were low, and in the absence of the River Pride, other lions took the opportunity to cross the river below Headquarters One.

First, two females from a pride across the river attempted the feat, using rocks jutting out of the water as stepping stones before cautiously paddling through the cold water, snarling and hissing in distaste and fear. They'd been attracted by the smell of blood from a hippo carcass killed by three of Kali's companions right below Headquarters One. Next, one of these males crossed and re-crossed the river in the same place; and later on, Kali himself did the same. Exciting as it was to see, we missed seeing the River Pride in their heartland and worried that they'd lost control of their core area.

Just as we'd given up hope, our spotters called in early July to say they thought they'd found the Pride. They were a long way from their usual haunts so we weren't at all sure it was them. Not only that, but we dreaded seeing who had managed to survive and who had not.

We traveled fifteen kilometers downriver to cross the lower bridge that spans the Mara River. We left the Mara Conservancy behind and headed deep into the Narok County Council's side of the reserve. We found the spotters' car parked next to a half-eaten wildebeest with another untouched carcass stashed at the base of a fig tree, deep in a gully. The lions were sleeping heavily in the midst of thick clumps of waving grasses, and we couldn't see any of them properly.

Anxious minutes went by before we could confirm it was indeed the River Pride. Soon we could account for the three adult females and some of the youngsters. But none of them was Mara—she was one of the most recognizable with a telltale nick in her ear. As time went by, one after another lifted their heads, and we still didn't see her. She was almost the last to lift her head, but she was there, right in the middle of the pride. Before leaving, we were able to do a full head count—all the other seven youngsters were there too. For the first time in months, we relaxed. The River Pride had made it through the weeks of turbulence. Since they'd done this well so far, we even allowed ourselves to hope that the adult females would keep one step ahead of Kali and his gang, ensuring that Mara and the other youngsters would make it through to adulthood.

PAGES 126–129: After eight months' absence, the arrival of huge wildebeest herds was a welcome relief for the River Pride and all the other lions in the reserve.

OPPOSITE PAGE: In the absence of the River Pride, intruding lions started to regularly cross the river below Headquarters One; first were females (**top**) then Kali himself (**bottom**).

PAGES 132–133: When we finally caught up with the River Pride, it was a relief to see them looking so relaxed and healthy.

Sita's cubs were now approaching the time when they would have to leave their mother. In August 2009, the cheetah cubs reached their first birthday and were nearly the same size as their mother, making it harder to tell who was who. Each cub still had a distinct fluffy ruff on the back of her neck, and if you looked closely, they still had cublike faces, but otherwise they could easily be mistaken for adult cheetahs.

With such large cubs, Sita could travel quickly, often moving five or six kilometers a day. The cubs' behavior had also changed dramatically. They were no longer bystanders when Sita hunted. Now they tried to play a part in the process—rarely with the desired results. Cheetah cubs at this age want to chase everything, from the attainable to the completely unattainable. This latter category includes animals far too big to ever contemplate bringing down—like adult wildebeests and adult topi—and sometimes includes even the ridiculous, like the very dangerous buffalo.

Initially, the buffalo would appear disconcerted when they noticed that they were being stalked by the little cats. But they would quickly go onto the offensive when they realized that these were just cheetah cubs threatening them. Fortunately, the agile young cheetahs were in little danger when the buffalo charged back, as they could easily dodge or outrun a cumbersome buffalo. But we did question the wisdom of provoking such a notoriously grumpy and threatening animal.

All young cats at this age seem to go through a period of testing the most dangerous animals they can find. It is probably not just a game, but more an important part of preparing for independence. By testing themselves with potential enemies, they learn how each opponent may react and their limits. Later in life, if they are ever taken by surprise by these dangerous beasts, they will instantly know how to cope. In the Mara, knowing your enemies is a crucial survival skill. Sita probably learned how she could goad lions and hyenas at this age, and this experience later allowed her to save her cubs.

When the cubs decided to hunt something of a sensible size, they usually got it terribly wrong. They had learned the basics of stalking and would go through the motions of a slow crouched walk as they sneaked toward their target. However, they certainly had not mastered the art of patience. Usually,

By now the cubs were a year old and nearly the same size as their mother. Their nervousness was a thing of the past. Instead, they now seemed to want to challenge every animal on the plains.

they charged far too early and would blow their chances in a moment of poor judgment. Even when Sita led the hunt, stalking as the consummate professional she was, the cubs would start to stalk with her but then ruin her opportunity with a reckless charge. These errors can become a serious danger for a cheetah family, as the four adult-size cheetahs needed to successfully hunt at least every other day. If Sita started to struggle to catch her prey, the whole family could quickly be in trouble.

Fortunately, the period of ineptitude was short. Once the cubs finessed their stalking, the family became a truly formidable force. Being run down by one cheetah was difficult enough for a gazelle, but being chased by a pack of four was a fearsome prospect. At this point, the fortunes of our cheetah family really did change. Those dark, dangerous early days of the year before felt like a distant memory. Now the cheetah family seemed confident and in control.

The adolescent cubs endlessly chased the numerous antelope in the Mara, but their attentions were also drawn to other predators. If they saw a jackal, a diminutive foxlike scavenger, they would leap into action, chasing the little dog as it yapped with indignity. If they caught up with it, they would try to trip it, bowling the jackal over, but then their attack would stop. Occasionally, the jackals turned on the cheetahs, snapping at their heels with sharp teeth. The young cheetahs were not so keen when the tables were turned.

OPPOSITE PAGE: The cubs now took the lead when hunting, but they still had a lot to learn. They would usually begin the chase too soon, alerting their prey before they were close enough to catch it. Their mother still had one last lesson to teach them: patience.

ABOVE: If the cubs stumbled across a jackal, they were now bold enough to chase it. But the irritated jackal would not take well to this, barking and bearing its teeth at the cheetah cubs. The cubs, though, would flee before any harm could come to them.

In longer grass, Sita's family would occasionally come across a serval cat. These are one of the smaller cat species in the Mara. Servals are beautifully elegant spotted cats, standing about half a meter high on long thin legs, and they are predominantly rodent and bird hunters. They are "pounce" predators, ambushing their prey rather than running in long chases. So when Sita's cubs took on a serval one day, all the poor little cat could do was turn and try to defend itself. Again, sharp teeth probably kept the cheetah cubs at bay, but as the three cubs circled and hounded the smaller cat, it felt reminiscent of the day when the cheetah brothers bullied Sita. Suddenly, we felt true sympathy for the serval. It was strange to see the cheetah family as the aggressors rather than the victims, and it was a sharp reminder that they are wild animals in a harsh and dangerous world. What might seem cruel to us was just another stage in their learning to survive in this challenging environment. Fortunately, no lasting harm ever came to any serval they chose to bully.

One animal the cheetah cubs did not chase was the hyena. An adult hyena weighs twice as much as a female cheetah and has bone-crushing jaws that all of Africa fears. Hyenas often look like sleepy, benign creatures, but never let their appearance deceive. They switch to killer mode in an instant, and only lions have the power to take them on. So Sita's cubs remained cautious of hyenas, but like their mother, they now stood their ground rather than escaping up a tree, arching their backs and hissing in defiance as long as food was not involved. When hyenas caught the cheetah family eating a gazelle, the whole family quickly gave way and handed over their dinner. Hyenas were just too dangerous to fight.

The cubs' other nemesis in their early days was still the lion. As Sita continued her journey on her endless hunt for gazelles, she was always in lion territory. Now that she was close to Paradise Plain, she was in the heart of Kali's kingdom, the home of the first pride he and his sons took over. But this did not seem to worry Sita. On many days, she and the cubs lay under one tree, while Kali or some of his sons slept a few hundred meters away under another. Sita had learned how to live among lions, and now that the cubs were so agile, she seemed almost relaxed with lions nearby. If the best hunting was in the middle of Kali's land, then that was where Sita would be. Keeping the food coming was now her biggest priority, and she was not going to let a few lions get in the way of this mission.

Conflict with Kali's pride was inevitable, but nothing could have prepared us for the way it would happen. One cloudy morning in September, the three cheetah cubs were sitting up, shoulder to shoulder, looking intently toward a croton thicket. Their ears were up and their stares were unwavering. Sita sat a few yards away, looking completely disinterested.

Serval cats are a common cat in the Masai Mara. They are relatively small, hunting rodents and birds rather than gazelles.

Then we noticed what had caught the cubs' attention. A lioness from Kali's main pride, neighbors of the River Pride, had emerged, and walking behind her were three tiny lion cubs. For a minute or two, the cheetah cubs continued to stare, but then one set off in a stalk toward the lioness and her cubs. The other cheetah cubs quickly followed, as did a bemused Sita. The cubs were going on a lion hunt! But this was not a defensive maneuver like Sita had done in the past. This appeared very offensive.

As the lioness meandered casually across the open ground, with a trail of tiny cubs behind her, the cheetah family slowly stalked forward. We had never witnessed anything like this. The lioness didn't seem to notice the approaching cheetahs. Closer and closer the cheetahs came, and now this was starting to look dangerous as even one lioness is more than a match for four cheetahs. The moment the lioness looked up at the cheetahs, they instantly froze like statues, but as soon as the lioness looked away, they continued their creep forward. The lioness ambled into another thicket with her cubs following, and as they disappeared, the cheetahs finally seemed to lose interest. Lions had clearly become a fascination to the cubs. But our concern was: would curiosity kill the cat?

OPPOSITE PAGE: Sita's cubs were becoming increasingly inquisitive, rather than fearful, of lions.

ABOVE: Kali's original pride, north of the river, had given birth to many small cubs. Sita's emboldened cubs had a dangerous fascination with Kali's newborns.

Throughout August 2009, we struggled to find Mara or any of the other lions, and our hearts sank. Out of nineteen lions at the beginning, the River Pride had been reduced to three adult females and seven youngsters plus Mara. Now even these few had disappeared again and, once more, we feared the worst. Another week flew past and there was still no sign of any of them. The wildebeest herds were scattered throughout the reserve, and it was the biggest, most spectacular migration in years. On our journeys, we often came across long lines of wildebeests snaking across the horizon or flattened paths curving into the distance over the plains as they'd moved through in the night, trampling the long grasses in search of fresh forage.

While the reserve still had much to offer the herds, it was a different story elsewhere in Kenya. Very dry for the second year running, the crops and grazing had withered all over the country with cattle, sheep, and goats dying by the thousands. During this time, Kenyan pastoralists lost eighty to ninety percent of their livestock, a truly shocking occurrence.

This news, combined with no sightings of any of our lions, made the days seem bleak indeed. Finally, we received reports from a driver on the Mara Conservancy side of the river that some young lions had been found. We quickly moved there, but it took four days before we saw some of the lions for ourselves.

We found three of the five young males but the next day, there was no sign of these. However, some three kilometers away, we caught up with the three adult females from the River Pride. They weren't alone—Kali and one of his gang were lying nearby, staring at them in what we felt to be a proprietary fashion. During the past weeks, we'd often be in our camp at night, listening to roars of three or more of these big males as they prowled the plains in search of the females. It seemed that after months of intensifying pressure, the females had finally succumbed, and the takeover we'd feared for so long had occured.

Initially, the three females were wary, even aggressive with the new males, but as the days passed, they relaxed a little. And after a time, the females began to return with the males to Headquarters One where once we'd delighted in seeing Fang reign supreme during his glory days.

We traveled several kilometers every day but found it increasingly hard to find any members of the pride.

September came and we were searching for Mara. Understandably, if she was still alive, she and the other youngsters would be in hiding since they were in grave danger from Kali and his cohorts. We divided our time between looking for the youngsters and for the adult females, and one day something totally unexpected happened. The three adult females were on their own, feeding on an impala carcass, when three other lionesses made a dramatic entrance. Two were met with snarls and blows but one was not. Looking at this one closely, we suddenly realized it was Grumpy Gran. We hadn't seen her for four months so we'd assumed she was dead. It was wonderful to see her alive and well, but what was she doing with two strange lionesses?

Our experiences in the past had taught us that lionesses don't change prides or allegiances so we were mystified until a local safari guide told us that some years before, a large pride had split in half, part of which became the River Pride. Grumpy Gran was much older than the other three females in the River Pride and might have been alive at the time of the split. Maybe she'd been able to leave the River Pride in order to join the splinter group for a few months, and perhaps this temporary transfer in allegiance had enabled her to keep out of Kali's way.

However, from this day on, Grumpy Gran rejoined the River Pride without a backward look, and by early October it was obvious that she was pregnant. A few weeks later, she gave birth in the gardens of Serena Lodge. It was good news, and we hoped this marked a shift in the tide for the River Pride's fortunes.

PAGES 144–145: Four months after Fang's disappearance, the adult females of the River Pride started to mate with Kali and other members of his gang.

ABOVE: After the takeover, the youngsters continued to be well-fed, and we thought the adult females were still managing to help them catch food at night.

OPPOSITE PAGE: The River Pride's adult females didn't tolerate strangers anywhere near their kill.

Just as Grumpy Gran reappeared in the pride's life, Mara and the other youngsters emerged from hiding. They were still very cautious and hard to find, but it was deeply satisfying to be able to locate them far more regularly than before. Rarely, though, did we see all eight youngsters together and what groupings there were seemed haphazard and random. Occasionally, one or more of the adult females would be with them. We began to suspect that the females were even helping feed them since the youngsters often had relatively full tummies in the morning. Kali's takeover wasn't turning out to be as clear-cut as we'd first imagined, but to our young lions, these big males remained a lurking menace, often appearing without warning on the skyline. Whenever this happened, the adult females would stay still, waiting for the males to arrive—we even thought they might be acting as decoys—while the youngsters rushed off, not daring to stop until they were two, even three kilometers away.

There was one day, though, when we found Mara and the seven other youngsters playing. Running around, their tails waving in the air, they were pouncing, wrestling, and leaping on each other. It was a wonderful few minutes. We hadn't seen them look so joyful for months, and we hoped their future was bright. In reality, the world was closing in on them.

On November 16, a year to the day after we'd first met them, we found all eight youngsters huddled together. This time, there was no attempt at play. Instead, they looked strangely unwell. The next day, we thought they were dying. Whenever they tried to stand, their legs shook with convulsions. Some were vomiting. By this time, there'd been so many reports in Kenyan papers about lions and other carnivores being poisoned on the edge of the reserve and elsewhere in the country. Poisoning might have explained their condition. By mid-morning, most of them weren't moving.

Then we noticed some had blood in their diarrhea and this, we knew, indicated food poisoning, maybe from scavenging off rotten meat. We had not seen them with the adult females for some time and guessed that they'd probably eaten the bad meat in desperation; it was a terrible sign for the future. Luckily, by the next day, their eyes were bright and they'd stopped convulsing. Even so, it took them another three days to fully recover.

After this, though we never saw any of the adult females with them ever again, Mara and the other youngsters formed a cohesive group, and we found them fairly regularly. However, adversity struck soon after this once more. One of Mara's female companions appeared with a wound on her haunch that was so deep we could see right inside to the severed muscle. She tried to lie on it as much as possible, to keep the flies away, and was licking it to keep it clean. Incredibly, she wasn't limping; she didn't even seem to be in pain.

Tusks and horns tend to rip and tear muscles and flesh, but this was such a localized wound with muscle so cleanly and deeply sliced that it looked as if she might have run afoul of a blade of some kind. Since the drought had become worse throughout Kenya, herders were bringing cattle to graze into the edge of the reserve, close to where our lions would sometimes wander. None of our young lions would have had any experience with herdsmen before, and they may have unwittingly gotten too close for comfort. Although the Maasai have lived alongside lions for centuries, there are sometimes conflicts when lions come too close to herds. Understandably, some may be speared to protect the herds, and this was a possible explanation for the lioness's wound.

Sadly, there are signs that the lion population in and around the Masai Mara National Reserve may have declined in recent years. This is similar to the situation throughout their range in Africa. Across the continent, the lion population has plummeted in both protected and non-protected areas. There are all sorts of reasons, such as a decrease in prey availability coupled with loss of habitat; and increase in disease, political instability, and direct conflict with local people. Lions have already lost eighty-three percent of their historical range in Africa; it would be devastating for them to lose even more.

Lions in the reserve face other problems, as made clear by an incident the month before our arrival in August 2008, when a lioness was found dead in a snare set by poachers not far from our camp in the Mara Conservancy. Snares are the wildlife equivalent of landmines, and poachers set them around the Mara every day to kill and maim animals in order to supply an escalating trade in illegal bush meat. However, the poachers don't have it all their way. We spent time on a patrol organized by the Mara Conservancy to remove snares just outside the Mara's border. In a small area of forty square kilometers, and in the space of a mere three hours, the rangers removed nearly 200 snares. Since one in seven snares catches an animal, this morning patrol alone saved thirty or so. Nine lucky wildebeests were also released alive, but we found it sobering to come across the grisly remains of twenty-one that had been caught and butchered the night before.

It should be emphasized that the Masai Mara National Reserve is a well-protected habitat for animals, including lions and cheetahs. Problems occur in the less-protected areas on the boundary of the reserve, but fortunately even here there are rays of light. Various conservancies are being created on the borders of the reserve where a percentage of the tourist revenue from regulated operators will be paid directly to the local people. As a result, it may well pay them to protect both predators and prey while reducing the number of cattle, goats, and sheep. That will be vital for the health of the vegetation, all sorts of grazing animals and, therefore, lions and cheetahs. For out of the nineteen or so prides in the reserve, only five stay within its boundaries all the time, and nearly all the female cheetahs range outside the reserve at some time in their lives. So linking protected and non-protected areas both here and elsewhere in Africa will be vital in the years to come.

However, while weighty matters such as the long-and-short-term risks and perils facing our lions and cheetahs could occupy our minds for hours, Mara and her friends lay resting in blissful ignorance. The young female's wound was healing well, and it was December. Once more, the wildebeest and zebra herds were leaving the reserve, and lean times were coming. Since the adult females had found it hard enough to manage last year, we had no idea how such inexperienced youngsters would be able to make it on their own.

PAGE 149 and OPPOSITE PAGE: A year after we'd started following them, the youngsters became very ill. Huddled together out in the open, all of them were too weak to move—even with the arrival of inquisitive hyenas.

PAGES 152–153: Many thousands of wildebeests are caught by poachers every year but the Mara Conservancy sends out regular patrols to pick up snares and release any live wildebeest that may have been caught. In this way, dozens of lives are saved while the herds of zebras and wildebeests also experience more peace in the Conservancy than they would otherwise.

These were difficult times, and matters were about to become very worrisome once again for Sita and our cheetah family. The three cheetah brothers continued to patrol their territory, scent-marking the bigger trees, driving off rivals, and harassing any female who strayed onto their land. They too were a year older, and at nearly five years of age looked even bigger and more powerful. These were three cheetah males in their prime.

Sita had spent much of her time skirting the edges of the brothers' territory, and we rarely saw her in the heart of their land. This could have been because the hunting there was poor, but after her earlier experiences, we suspected that she may well have been avoiding them. With their continual scent-marking, she would have found it easy to know whenever she was entering their territory.

At its southern end, the brothers' land overlapped with Kali's territory. The brothers always appeared very nervous of lions. They knew too much to show any of Sita's cubs' curiosity in these great adversaries. If the brothers ever saw a lion, they headed off rapidly in the opposite direction. However, scent-marking duty demanded that they venture into the pride area from time to time. On one of their visits, Sita was hunting the same patch. A meeting this time would be very different than their first encounter. The cubs were nearly full-grown, and Sita could be ready to mate.

As Sita and her cubs weaved across the cheetah brothers' territory, another encounter seemed inevitable.

On this clear, sunny morning, the cheetah brothers were harassing herds of topi, looking for newborn fawns. Sure enough, they found what they were looking for and rushed in for the kill. Topi mothers aggressively defend their young, charging at the predators as a bull does a matador. A few days earlier, Sita and the cubs were forced away from a baby topi by its very aggressive mother. But the brothers were too big to be bullied by a distraught topi mother, and while two of them concentrated on driving her off, the third secured the meal. It was a well-practiced piece of teamwork and a sharp reminder of the power of the cheetah brothers.

Sita and the cubs were almost a kilometer away from where the brothers made their kill, distracted by chasing a warthog family. It was Sita who first spotted the approaching cheetah brothers as they trotted across the plain in her direction. The distracted cubs only realized the danger when the brothers were in full charge, hurtling at them through the long grass. The chase was on, but Sita and the cubs never stood a chance of escape. As the attackers knocked the cheetah girls to the ground, the situation became chaotic with seven similar-looking cheetahs fighting in the long grass. The brothers seemed to concentrate their attack on Sita, but the cubs also took a beating.

Eventually, the brothers retreated, and two of the cubs decided to make a run for it. Sita stayed put with her third cub, and then started to call for the other two to join her. Unfortunately, the calls brought back the brothers instead. Once again, they attacked Sita and the lone cub. In the confusion, the lone cub bolted, with all three of the brothers in hot pursuit. Sita could only watch helplessly as her cub fled with the brothers close on her tail.

As the lone cub and the brothers ran south, Sita set off to find the other two cubs that had run to the north. The family was split, running in opposite directions. To our relief, Sita soon found her other two cubs, and all three continued north. To the south, the brothers soon caught up with the terrified and isolated cub. They quickly realized that she was too young to mate, and a standoff ensued. The poor cub was exhausted, with foam in her mouth caused by excessive panting from having run so far in the heat of the day. She slowly retreated to a rocky ridge while the brothers found some shade to recover from their exertion. The lone cub was now at least five kilometers from her mother and sisters, and our team had to split to follow the lost cub and Sita. Never before had the family been separated so widely.

No matter how many times we had seen Sita bring her family back from the brink of disaster, we worried that our cheetah family might never be reunited and that something terrible might happen to the lone, inexperienced cub who was still too young to fend for herself. Soon the afternoon storm clouds began to build. To our relief, the lost cub started heading north

OPPOSITE PAGE, TOP: When the migrating herds of wildebeests head south, topi are one of the few antelope that remain in the Mara. Topi are usually too big for a female cheetah such as Sita to hunt, but the cheetah brothers can bring one down.

OPPOSITE PAGE, BOTTOM: When the cheetah brothers attacked, it became very confusing with seven cheetahs fighting in the long grass.

ABOVE: Sita and her two remaining cubs were very agitated after the encounter with the cheetah brothers.

OPPOSITE PAGE: One of Sita's cubs became separated from the family during the cheetah brothers' assault. Worryingly, it seemed she might never be reunited with her mother.

in the direction of Sita and the other cubs. She gave the brothers a wide berth and somehow knew the exact direction in which to walk in order to find her mother and sisters. We often witnessed cat cubs—lions, leopards, or cheetahs—knowing just where to go to find their families. We thought perhaps this was thanks to smell, but on this occasion, Sita's cub took a different route than the retreating family had, and so she could not have been following a scent trail. Eventually, her homing methods worked, and as the evening rain fell, Sita's family was reunited.

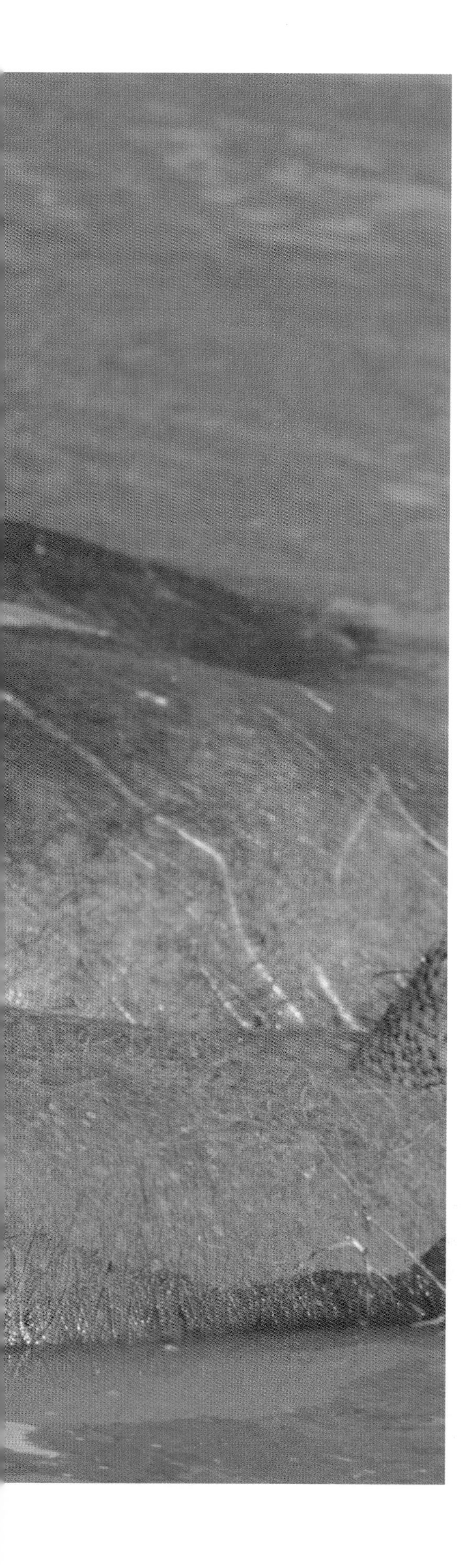

A few days later, Sita went on one of her longest journeys yet. We speculated that she had had more than enough of the brothers and was getting well away from their scented territory. But who will ever know the true workings of a cheetah mind?

Sita and her family first headed east, then turned south and marched toward the Tanzanian border. Here, the Masai Mara National Reserve becomes the Serengeti National Park: a meaningless border to a cheetah, but for us a huge barrier. The nearest legal crossing point involves a round trip of hundreds of kilometers, along with all the logistical difficulties of setting up another filming operation in a remote part of another country. If Sita had continued into Tanzania, we would certainly have lost her and all our contact with the cheetah family's dramatic life. That would have been the end of our story. Luckily, she turned west and headed straight for the bank of the Mara River.

Kenya's drought had intensified. Even the Mara was dusty and the sun-scorched grass had been grazed to a short stubble by the hordes of migrating wildebeests and zebras that had poured onto the last patch of land with any grazing left. The Mara River was lower than any of us could remember, largely due to the lack of rainfall at its source, but also due to the scale of agricultural irrigation and deforestation upstream. This had burgeoned in recent years and was now taking its toll. The Mara River is the lifeblood of this unique reserve and the northern Serengeti, and seeing it this low was a concern for the future. Maintaining the balance between providing for the needs of the Mara's wildlife and for those of Kenya's agriculture was becoming increasingly difficult; the state of the river was just one indication that all was not well. Fortunately the warning signs have been heeded and a multimillion-dollar project has just begun to save the upriver Mau forest, which provides the watershed to the mighty Mara River.

The fact that the Mara River's usual rapid current had slowed almost to a standstill was a bonus for Sita. The cheetah family first patrolled the high bank, stopping to stare into the river's deeper pools, now full of hippos seeking out the last of the deep water. Lying on the banks was the usual gathering of giant crocodiles. Cheetahs are even more vulnerable than the lions to crocodile attacks, and they clearly knew all about the dangers as they hissed at the giant reptiles whenever they saw one. For people, crossing this river would be a terrifying prospect. We can only surmise that the cheetah family felt the same way.

The steep banks of the Mara are broken by little gullies, carved out by the

hippo herds as they leave the river every night to graze on the open plains. The cheetahs used one of these hippo gullies to walk down to the water's edge. There they stared at the hippos, transfixed by these huge animals lying in the water just a few feet away. This was no place to cross, as the harmless-looking hippos can attack even grazing animals that choose to swim too close. They would not take kindly to a cat family swimming through their midst. So Sita led the family upstream. Cheetahs rarely approach rivers, and the family looked extremely uncomfortable so close to the water's edge.

They were very tense and nervous, jumping at the slightest disturbance and constantly looking into the water for any sign of danger. When they reached a relatively hippo-free section of the river, Sita stopped and stared into the water for well over an hour. It must have been the crocodiles she was looking for, and we shared her worry. Crocodiles can remain submerged and invisible for very long periods. An apparently crocodile-free stretch of African river is no assurance that death is not seconds away if you unwisely get too close to the water's edge.

Eventually, Sita and her family waded a short distance into the river to a stranded log, before peering again into the deep dark water. The family seemed to be perched by the log for ages before starting to move to a small rock a meter or so ahead. As they waded forward, one of the cubs lost her footing and began to drift away in the current. She now had to swim, and the others had no choice: Sita and the remaining two cubs leaped in, and the whole family swam and splashed across the river as fast as they could. As they scrambled up the opposite bank, we certainly shared their relief. Now we understood why cheetah families rarely cross this river. But Sita's caution had paid off. Her intense scrutiny of the crossing point had insured that the family was not attacked by crocodiles.

Cheetahs have rarely been seen crossing large rivers; if they do, it can increase their "home hunting range" considerably. Sita clearly knew where and when to cross, and this may have been another important lesson for her now almost-adult cubs.

PAGE 160: Hippos inhabit the Mara River, with a large herd in most of the river's pools. Hippos are grazers, but despite this, they can be very aggressive animals.

OPPOSITE PAGE: Cheetahs have rarely been seen to cross large rivers like the Mara. Crocodiles are known to attack even the big cats, and Sita seemed well aware of the danger. Having spent several hours looking for a crocodile-free section of the river, the whole family finally crossed safely.

PAGES 164–165: The storm clouds signaled that troubled times lay ahead for our young lions.

In contrast to Sita's happy family, we knew Mara and the seven other lion youngsters now had no guidance from their mothers or even aunts and frustratingly, they'd once again melted into the undergrowth so we had no idea how they were getting on. As we'd followed the various members of the pride over the last year, we'd discovered bit by bit that the pride's home range spanned both sides of the river and measured about twenty by six kilometers. That meant we had some 120 square kilometers to search, including deep and impenetrable woodlands, impassable rocky ridges, thick vegetation along the riverbanks, and innumerable thickets.

Sometimes finding the youngsters again felt impossible so we felt particularly triumphant when we finally caught sight of the five young males. But our excitement was short-lived. As the group stood up, we noticed one of them had wounds on his abdomen and hind leg that were far, far worse than the young female's wound that we'd seen a few weeks before. They were so bad that we simply couldn't understand how he was still alive.

Only a buffalo, we guessed, could have caused such a massive injury, and this reminded us of something that the safari guides had told us about finding the young lions eating buffalo carcasses in our absence. We'd never seen their mothers hunt buffalo and had assumed that they'd been finding ailing and dying buffalo weakened by the drought.

But we were wrong since not long afterward, we saw three young males, including the injured one, harassing a healthy female buffalo with a newborn calf. She kept them at bay until eight other buffalo joined in to chase the lions away. Now it seemed entirely feasible that the youngsters had been trying to hunt sound and strong buffalo when this one had been injured. The young males were only fourteen months old and nowhere near strong or experienced enough to tackle such animals. It was a futile and desperate endeavor born out of hunger and relatively few other animals to hunt.

Luckily, the injured youngster could reach his wounds to lick them and keep them clean. As the days went past, we managed to keep up with this little group of five males and discovered that they had developed into expert scavengers, quick to spot vultures diving down to the ground—a dead giveaway that there were remains of a kill.

At night, we guessed, the group was probably strong enough to muscle in and steal food from small groups of hyenas. But fighting for their living came at a cost. Our once-fine young males were turning into battle-scarred beasts that were lean and hungry all the time. Luckily the injuries caused by

the buffalo didn't seem to be getting worse, but one morning we discovered one of that lion's companions harpooned with porcupine quills that stuck out at rakish angles from his face and below his chin, testimony to an unhappy experience the night before.

While the young males were struggling in this way, we wondered what on earth had happened to Mara. The rains had finally come, and the whole of Kenya was green with grass, and at last the cows left the reserve. At least we had one less thing to worry about on her behalf. Our main preoccupation was how she would be getting enough food to eat now or in the weeks to come. There were still three to four months before the wildebeest and zebra herds normally arrived. This year, the rains had been so good in Tanzania that the herds might come later; they might not even come at all. After everything that had happened to Mara so far, we couldn't bear to think that starvation would be her end.

Meanwhile, the number of adult females in the River Pride had increased once more since the lioness that had gone missing in June, at the same time as Grumpy Gran and Fang, had also, inexplicably, turned up. In her absence, she might have been living on her own or had joined the same pride as Grumpy Gran. Whatever happened, the River Pride was back up to its full complement of five adult lionesses, but they weren't back in top form. Grumpy Gran, who had given birth to four cubs near Serena Lodge, was left with just one cub, and she was close to abandoning it. The last time we saw it, it had somehow managed to find the five young males and was trying, hopelessly, to suckle from one of them. Other females in the pride had also become pregnant, but soon after giving birth, we'd see them mating again. However, we'd never see their cubs. Soon their milk would dry up, which meant their newborn cubs had been killed. Sadly, everyone in the River Pride was having a harder time than we could have imagined when we started following them in November 2008.

PAGE 167: The youngster's horrific wounds were the result, we thought, of the inexperienced lions, driven by hunger, trying to catch buffalo—prey so dangerous that even their mothers and Fang had avoided hunting them.

PAGES 168–169: One of the young females was in much better shape than the young males; we hoped that it was the same case for Mara but had no idea where she was or how she was getting on.

OPPOSITE PAGE: Our little group of young lions still faced three to four months of hunger and hardship before the return of the wildebeest herds.

Fortunately, life for the cheetah family was brighter. After their dramatic river crossing, the family initially moved quickly across the Mara Conservancy, land that was completely new to the cubs. Each day, Sita took the cubs on long journeys, skirting the Tanzanian border and then moving northwest, deep into the conservancy. The cubs' hunger was insatiable, and the family hunted every day. At this age and size, a family of four cheetahs will eat an adult Thomson's gazelle one day and look lean and hungry the next, ready to hunt another. The cubs had become competent hunters, nearly always leading the way in the stalk and then charging as a team at the unfortunate prey. Nowhere was their teamwork more apparent than when they turned their attention to hunting reedbuck.

Reedbuck are secretive antelope, usually living on their own or in pairs. Close to the high rocky walls of the Mara escarpment, which forms the western border of the National Reserve, there is an area dotted with Balanites trees and numerous low-lying shrubby bushes. This is ideal reedbuck country, with these antelope often hiding during the day, tucked up on the edge of the bushes. The cheetah family could not see the reedbuck in the distance, as they would have with their usual gazelle prey, so they adopted a different hunting strategy. They would spread out across the open woodland, sniffing at every bush with hope of surprising a hiding buck.

Often, it was the cub farthest ahead that would find the hiding prey. Once flushed out, the buck would rush to escape, but more often than not ran straight into the other charging cubs and Sita. The whole cooperative hunt was ruthlessly efficient, and nearly every hunt ended with the capture of a reedbuck.

Now that Sita and her cubs were on the other side of the river, they were no longer separated from Kali and his partners; by this time, the lion gang spent just as much time to the south of the river as they did to the north. One evening, Sita and the cubs walked straight into one of Kali's sons, and we expected high drama. It was anything but, as the plucky young cheetahs treated him almost with contempt. The lumbering lion chased after the young cheetahs as they danced around him. It was clear that Sita had done her job well: these cubs could handle the most dangerous carnivore in the Mara. We were confident that with their hunting and survival skills honed, Sita's cubs were ready for independence.

As we watched this pack of cheetahs hunting, and observed their incredible success rate, we had to wonder why adult female cheetahs are such solitary animals, unlike lions who hunt in prides. Ultimately, the answer

is probably because it is simply more efficient. A group of cheetahs may be successful, but all of them have to expend energy in the chase, and then they have to share the meal. A solitary cheetah need only hunt every three or four days, and the rest of the time can relax and conserve her energy. Interestingly, the cats that do stay and hunt in groups, like male cheetahs and lion prides, also have to defend territories against rivals. Females like Sita do not need to hold any ground. It is probably the need for defense that forces male cheetahs and lions together rather than the potential advantages when hunting as a pack. Hence even solitary lionesses tend to have little problem hunting on their own, but without a pride's protection, they rarely succeed in raising cubs to adulthood.

PAGE 173: With the plains largely empty, Sita took her cubs close to the Mara escarpment, in search of reedbuck. The Balanites trees and scrubby bushes that dot this area make it ideal territory for reedbuck.

OPPOSITE PAGE: Now that Sita's cubs were nearly adults, they were bursting with confidence. Even lions did not scare them—rather than run away, the youngsters would now wander closer to them, watching them intently.

ABOVE: Once their curiosity was satisfied, the cubs would cautiously slink away. The lions knew that chasing a cheetah was a futile exercise.

In mid-March 2010, we finally managed to find Mara again. She was with the two other young females, and these three had joined up with the five young males. Mara was the youngest and thinnest of the females, and the fact that she'd survived so far was nothing short of a miracle; we found it incredible that during the last few months, she'd been able to get enough food to eat.

For days, the eight youngsters barely moved from a grassy area that we called Tree Arch Plain, where they spent most of their time sleeping in the shade. The injured young male was the thinnest of all. Though his terrible wound was healing remarkably well, it had obviously taken its toll on his strength. Slowly, as time passed, we began to think that they'd lost the will to live. Prey was so hard to find and they were such young and inexperienced lions that it looked as if they were starving to death in front of our eyes. Uncomfortably, we began to feel like voyeurs. But we couldn't intervene; this was the result of a natural cycle of events.

However, when they managed to scavenge some scraps, we were elated. Often the only bits of a carcass left were pieces of skin and bone, and each individual grabbed what they could. Mara usually managed to get something, however small, and we realized that her genes were good; she had as much grit and determination as her mother, Layla, had displayed all those months ago.

Toward the end of the month, we found a termite mound at the base of which one of the young males was on his own, trying to dig out a warthog that had taken refuge down a hole. As they go underground, warthogs generally retreat backward, making sure their tusks face any intruder. Not only does a lion have to tackle cement-hard earth but knife-sharp tusks as well. But this young male was so hungry that he simply couldn't give up. Slowly and painstakingly, he scraped away at the soil until, inch by inch, he dug further and further into the hole. Hours later, only the tip of his back paw and tail could be seen. Even then, he couldn't reach the pig and stopped to take a breath. Emerging from the hole, he wobbled and nearly fell over, so weak that he could barely stand.

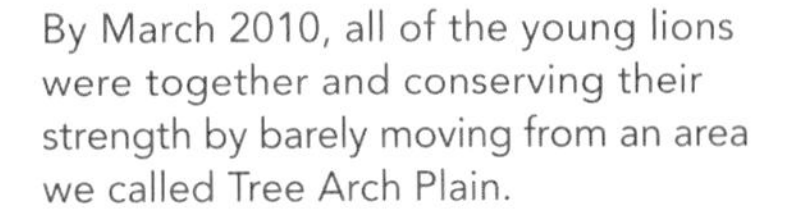

By March 2010, all of the young lions were together and conserving their strength by barely moving from an area we called Tree Arch Plain.

After a rest, he started again and this time disappeared from sight. When he came back up, his face was covered in blood and he was even chewing a little bit of meat. It had taken him two hours of hard work before reaping his rewards, so we could never pass this termite mound again without remembering his Herculean efforts.

It wasn't just this mound that was a familiar landmark for us. Cheetahs as well as lions had led us to many nooks and crannies, and since we'd been following them, we'd come to see some of the landscape through their eyes. One particular tree offered great shade and a wonderful vantage point, while the rocky area nearby was good for hunting and the gully offered a great opportunity to sneak up on the herds. However, though we might know their physical world better than we had at the beginning, Sita, the River Pride, and the youngsters still had plenty of surprises in store for us.

The young lions were thin and battle scarred yet, despite this, their tenacity to survive was undiminished.

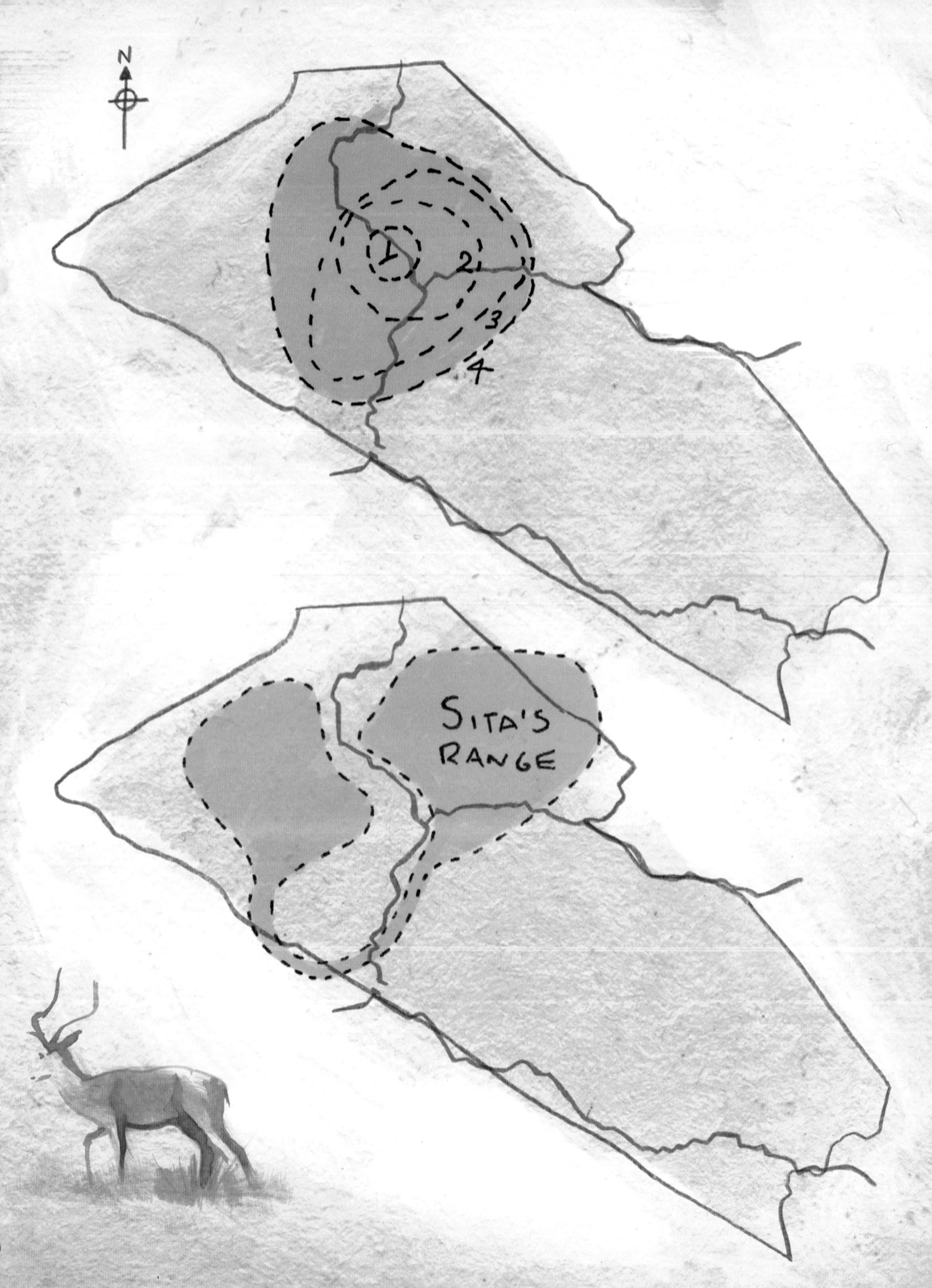
N
1
2
3
4
SITA'S
RANGE

MAP TWO

1. Pride's range October 2009–October 2010
2. Mara and the youngsters' range October 2009–October 2010
3. Pride's range October 2008–October 2009
4. Kali and his gang's range August 2008–October 2010

A surprise happened in our cheetah world in March 2010 when another cheetah mother, with a four-month-old cub, appeared in our area north of the river. She was an excellent hunter, chasing gazelles from extreme distances and nearly always succeeding. Her little cub had no siblings to play with, but her mother was very playful, unlike Sita who was always rather serious.

So who was this new cheetah? Again a trawl through the pictures of the cheetahs we had known, and their unique spot patterns, revealed her identity. And what a wonderful surprise it was. She was Duma, Sita's first daughter, whom we had known back in 2004. So this made the little cub Sita's granddaughter. This discovery confirmed beyond all doubt what a successful cheetah Sita was in the Mara—with not only three daughters about to leave her for independence, but with one of her earlier daughters successfully raising a cub of her own. Sita was building a dynasty of new cheetahs.

Success like this has far wider ramifications. Just fifty years ago, cheetahs were found across most of Africa's savannas and semi-desert regions. Each cheetah may need a huge area to support it, but if the overall area they can range in is vast, a healthy population can thrive. During the last half-century, this range has dramatically shrunk, due to human population increases and the corresponding growth in all aspects of agriculture. Some of our team grew up in Kenya, and even we can remember the time when most of Kenya's wildlife existed outside national parks and reserves. In a terrifyingly short time, most of Kenya's wildlife has become hemmed into sparse conservation areas, and the situation is the same or worse across the rest of Africa.

Relatively small conservation areas may suffice for animals that can live in high densities in small areas, but they may not be sufficient to support the long-term existence of wide roamers like the cheetahs. Sita and her descendants are fortunate to live in one of the largest conservation regions in Africa, as the combined area of the Serengeti and the Mara is some 30,000 square kilometers. But even this territory is under pressure with development around all the borders. Seeing a cheetah dynasty being built by Sita is evidence that for now, in this sanctuary at least, cheetahs can thrive.

One morning, we discovered a new female cheetah with a small cub. Wonderfully, we realized that the mother was one of Sita's cubs from an earlier litter. The arrival of the young cub meant that Sita was now a grandmother!

Later in March 2010, Sita finally separated from her three daughters. We were not there to witness this, but maybe that was a blessing. Having had the privilege to follow this family, from the time the cubs were tiny fluff balls to beautiful adults, is something none of us will ever forget or are likely to experience again. We all grew so close to the family, witnessing first-hand their ordeals, courage, and care for each other; it would have been heartbreaking to actually see the moment when Sita just turned and walked away. The cubs would have called for days for their mother before going their separate ways. It would have been very hard to watch.

For the cheetahs, we are now left with our powerful memories. Someday soon, we will return to the Mara and again go looking for cheetahs. You can be sure that we will carry our notes and sketches, and we will intently scrutinize any cheetah we see. Just imagine our joy if Sita or any of her three girls walks back into our lives!

OPPOSITE PAGE and ABOVE: At eighteen months old, the cubs were finally ready to fend for themselves. For a cheetah mother to raise a single cub to adulthood is a challenge; so for three healthy cubs to reach adulthood is a great success.

Everyone wants a happy ending, and we wanted exactly that for the lions. However, as March came and went, still none of the adult females in the River Pride had any new cubs joyfully bouncing beside them, and we could only speculate as to the reasons why.

Though Kali and his coalition looked magnificent to our eyes, they were probably bad news for the River Pride. As is the case with such large groups, the males had split up into different groupings of two or three. None of these stayed with the River Pride for longer than a few days. Instead, they wandered away after mating, moving back and forth between three or four prides. We thought it would be easy for one group to mate with the lionesses and then for the next group to kill the cubs, not knowing that they had been fathered by part of their own huge alliance. In their absence, we even saw strange males from outside moving through the area. The days of stability provided by Fang had long gone; and maybe the only hope was that some of Kali's coalition would settle with them long-term.

Meanwhile the young males were growing fast. Already they were a good few inches taller at the shoulder than Mara. But they were pathetically lanky; they just couldn't get enough nutrition to cope, and their rib and pelvic bones stuck out sharply through fur that had long lost its shine. Some days, we saw buffalo chase them and they didn't have the strength to do more than slowly trot away, glancing warily over their shoulders.

From late December 2009, the rain had been so heavy that the parched blonde landscape was now a brilliant, optimistic, blazing jade in color. All the grasses were thick, lush, and long. The red oat grass was in flower far earlier than usual, and as the sun sank low in the late afternoons, the seed heads shone a rich, burnished copper so that the rolling plains would turn a deep wine-red as far as the eye could see. But though they were a feast to our eyes, the plains were empty; the antelope, gazelles, and a few remaining zebras gathered on the rocky ridges where the grasses were shorter and they could keep a sharp lookout all around.

Despite the lack of easy prey, Kali and his companions were thriving. The males had become specialists in killing hippos at night, and though it must have been a particularly gory struggle, it gave them enough meat to last for days.

Crossing and recrossing the river to keep in touch with all three of their prides, they seemed inviolate. Then, one morning we found five of them walking and trotting together. At first they seemed to be merely in high spirits, but soon this turned to latent aggression and tension filled the air.

Kali seemed particularly wary of his companions, turning on them with a snarl and lunge if they got too close. His companions, some of whom may well have been his sons, walked together jostling each other roughly, their eyes transfixed on Kali. It was as if they were waiting and probing, ready to pounce on any sign of weakness. Kali had seemed invulnerable to us, but suddenly it seemed as though even he was living on borrowed time. There were so many other groups of males prowling on the edges of his kingdom, ready to take advantage of any weakness in the coalition's defenses.

Mara was still with the seven other youngsters, and suddenly it was brought home to us just how untenable their position was. Named after their home ranges, their immediate neighbors included the Ol Kiombo pride, the Ridge Pride, the Mara Bridge Pride, the Pumphouse Pride, and the M'goro Pride. The youngsters had hostile prides on every side. No wonder they were keeping together in the tiny area of Tree Arch Plain. Lions use soft contact calls to keep in touch with each other during the night or early mornings; or to find each other if one's been separated. If the youngsters attempted to call in this way, they ran the risk of attracting enemies. And one day that was what happened. It was in the heat of the midday sun when the land was wobbling in heat haze. To our horror, we caught sight of a big male sneaking up to Mara and the youngsters, inch by cautious inch, while they lay dozing in the shade of a bush. At the last minute they sensed him, and all except for one young male ran away. As the aggressor loomed over the thin youngster, we thought he'd be killed for sure. The big male pounced and though totally unprepared, the youngster turned and lashed out so fiercely that the big male backed off. The young male seized the moment to quickly run off to rejoin Mara and the others. But the unpleasant encounter reminded us that there was no safe haven in the Masai Mara for this small group of young lions.

The group stuck together for a few days until, suddenly, they split up with four of the young males going one way and one staying behind. We felt terribly bereft. After following them through thick and thin, we'd got to know them so well that we'd had names for each and every one of them. It was about the age that young males disperse to roam around before seeking a pride of their own, but we thought these youngsters were far too feeble to embark on such a dangerous journey. However, we'd have to wait and see. In the meantime, we watched as Dylan, the one left behind either by choice or accident, set off on a mission.

First he joined Mara and the two young females, and then the quartet intrepidly sought out the five adult females in the River Pride. It took an hour or two, but when they found them, the youngsters approached as quickly as they could, tails waving excitedly in the air. Immediately, most of the

PAGE 186: Buffalo usually chase lions whenever they come across them and when lions such as these are weakened by lack of food, there's no contest.

PAGES 188–189 and OPPOSITE PAGE: During the two years we'd followed the lions, we'd seen how Kali had gained a whole new lease on life.

ABOVE: Youngsters that had lost the rest of the group risked attracting unwelcome attention from Kali and his gang by calling in the hope of finding each other again.

OPPOSITE PAGE: Despite being five or six months younger, Mara was forming a close alliance with the other two young females in the group—a welcome sign for the future.

adults growled and laid their ears back flat on their heads, looking as surly as lions could be. Now, even the adult females of the River Pride had turned against them. Soon three of the adults disappeared back into thick bush at the bottom of a small gully, and the remainder relaxed, sleeping relatively close together all day. The next morning, Mara and her two female friends had vanished, and Dylan was alone with the five adult females. That day, his perseverance paid off. The group managed to catch one of the few zebras left behind when the herds migrated; and the adults tolerated his presence at the kill so he had his first big meal in months.

Obviously, Dylan thought his future was made and tried to hang around with the females for the next few days. One of his brothers, Zorro, even returned to join him. But a few days later, we found two of Kali's gang had come to pay the females a visit. The young males stayed at a distance peering warily at the group. The moment one of the big males moved to lie down in long grass, Dylan seized his chance to creep forward. He walked past the other big male who stared at him with what seemed to be total disbelief, but he surprisingly did nothing. Finally, after all of his efforts, one of the females allowed Dylan to rub heads with her. At that point, the other big male got up and stalked toward Dylan who remained oblivious of his impending approach. It looked as though Dylan's desire to be back with the River Pride females was a suicidal move. At the last minute as the big males loomed over him with deadly intent, the females ran away, and so did Dylan. We never saw any of the youngsters with the adult females again.

As the days hurtled toward the time for our departure at the end of April, we were desperate to find Mara. Then we had a lucky break. We found her and the two other young females with Dylan resting under a tree. A few hours later, a large antelope, rendered almost incapable of walking straight by a parasite in its brain, staggered past the tree. Mara and the others spotted a golden opportunity.

The three females killed the antelope swiftly, and joined by Dylan, enjoyed a much-needed bonanza of food. That evening, Mara's tummy was rounded and full; after so much struggle and loss, it was wonderful to see her looking at peace. She was still less than two years old, but she'd done well to survive so many months without the adult females. Now that she had developed close bonds with the other female youngsters, maybe the trio would, in time, be able to establish the nucleus of a pride of their own. Perhaps they could even rejoin the females of the River Pride. And, we reasoned, if such lucky moments as finding a sick antelope could happen out of the blue, her future was as assured as it ever could be.

Now, as the final number of filming days dwindled toward single figures, we did some calculations that neatly answered one of the questions people most often ask: namely, why do you need so much time in the field?

Out of the seventeen months between November 17, 2008 and April 24, 2010, we spent a total of 366 days on location with the River Pride. Working with specific lions meant that there were days when we couldn't find any of them, and these numbered eighty.

From the remaining 286 days, we had seventeen days that could be counted as significantly "good" filming days. For the rest, we either watched the lions sleeping or filmed something that helped make the scene work—a look, walking, running, a greeting, etcetera. The "good" days were, of course, totally unpredictable so we needed to go out in the bush seven days a week with the cars and cameras working perfectly or one of those precious days could slip past, never to be repeated.

Toward the end of filming, we discovered the lions still had the capacity to amaze us. The drama unfolded when we found Zorro and Dylan close to the river. It was still high after recent rains, and the youngsters spent a few minutes rubbing heads together gaining confidence from each other. Then one walked slowly down to the water's edge and paused, snarling at the water, watching the current rush past. He snarled again before walking into the water. Two steps more, and he was out of his depth. His head almost vanished underwater when, behind him, there was a splash and his young companion quickly paddled to join him. With their bodies touching, they swam out across one of the deadliest rivers in the world.

OPPOSITE PAGE: Two young males, Dylan and Zorro, swimming across the Mara River moments before the attack.

PAGE 197: Mara's tale had confounded and amazed us, but ultimately it was one of triumph and resilience in the face of adversity.

The rush of water was so strong that it carried them downstream, and they weren't able to make any headway. At moments like these, time seems to stand still, but in reality it was probably only twenty seconds or so and then they managed to beat the current. As they made it halfway, the second lion overtook the first, and as they separated, Zorro was dragged underwater by some unseen but incredible force. Our hearts stopped as we watched a heaving mass of empty water, but then his tail reappeared, flailing wildly as the struggle continued. It was a crocodile that was trying to drown him by pulling him underwater.

Dylan, looking absolutely terrified, jumped up out of the water and, glancing behind him, snarled. Then there was a sudden, desperate heave and Zorro, still wriggling and struggling to get free of his unseen foe, leaped out of the water too. Zorro finally managed to break out of the crocodile's grasp and both lions rushed for the safety of the bank in a glinting, arcing spray of water. Moments later, a crocodile surfaced and cruised up the river. The young lions had escaped death by a hair's breadth. The encounter had dramatically revealed the dangers that Mara, the other lions, and Sita's family had faced during their river crossings.

Many people have a saying that cats have nine lives, and in the last two years, we'd seen how this had been played out. Both Mara and Sita had survived close and sometimes terrifying encounters with their enemies in water and on land. Mara had also lost the support of her mother and then the pride and had survived food poisoning. By the skin of her teeth, she'd managed to avoid starving while keeping one step ahead of Kali and his gang.

For our part, following Mara, Sita, and the River Pride had by turns confounded, amused, saddened, amazed, and entertained us. We'd seen how resilient they had been when faced with misfortune and bad luck. From this we'd come to realize that such characters as Mara's mother, Mara herself, Fang, and Sita could appear to transcend their animal bonds in a world where the human rules of justice and fair play are in short supply.

It is, admittedly, an anthropocentric view. So when we'd looked deeply into their eyes, we wondered how they saw their world. They'd returned our gaze, seemingly without seeing us, but with such clarity and intensity of purpose that we felt refreshingly and totally inconsequential. The truth, though, is so very different. We are the dominant species, and ultimately their lives are held in our hands, their future wrapped up with ours. We hope that by sharing our insights about Mara, Sita, and the others in this book, we may promote empathy and increase respect as well as reinforce a desire to protect and conserve during the years to come. It's up to all of us to decide.

We returned to the Masai Mara in early July 2010 to get some extra shots needed to make the major scenes work well. We also wanted our happy ending. We found, despite the forecasts, that the wildebeest herds had arrived earlier than usual. The River Pride was down to just three adult females. Grumpy Gran and the other adult female were missing in the same way as they'd been the year before, so we hoped they'd return to the River Pride before too long. However, no driver or ranger had seen any of the young lions. We couldn't help but think that the lean weeks of May and early June had finally proved too much for them. And so it seemed for the first three weeks, until we had the best news we could hope for.

We found three young males living on the edge of the River Pride's home range on the Narok side of the Mara River, close to where the Pride had been this time last year. The group included Dylan as well as the one injured by the buffalo, whose wounds were now almost completely healed. They were fat and healthy, but how they'd survived was beyond our comprehension. Later, this group of three was joined by a fourth so, in the end, only one sub-adult male was missing. Now that the young males were more than two and one-half years old, we felt their survival skills had been honed in ways that couldn't be matched by other, more fortunate male youngsters, skills that would stand them in good stead for years to come. A day later, we found Mara and her two female companions sleeping peacefully under a bush not far, as the crow flies, from Headquarters One. We followed this little group of three for several weeks and found them to be adept at hunting wildebeests. We felt happier than words can say. We had seen how Mara, in particular, had navigated her way through her particularly stormy seas of adolescence with great aplomb. In real life, happy endings are rare, but for us, this was as close to a fairy-tale ending as one could hope for.

Sita and her cubs had not been seen in our filming area since soon after the family separated in March 2010. However, this was not cause for concern. The usual pattern for adolescent female cheetahs is to disperse after they leave their mother.

To the north of our filming area, outside the National Reserve, are the conservation areas on Maasai land. In early 2010, some of these conservancies started a huge effort to limit the cattle on the land in order to make more space for wildlife. Ten years ago, this area was the best place to find cheetahs, but as the livestock numbers grew, the cheetah numbers fell. However, since the actions taken to reduce the cattle, the cheetahs are returning, and this may well be where our youngsters and Sita have headed. These days, it is rare for new wild spaces to be created anywhere in the world, let alone in Africa. But in the Mara it is happening, thanks to the work of many dedicated local people. With efforts like these, Sita's and Mara's descendants will live on for generations to come, and the Masai Mara will remain one of Africa's most special wilderness areas for our big cats.

SEAN AVERY

A hydrologist, Sean was born in Tanzania and has lived in Kenya for all his professional life. He had little time to source and supervise the modifications of the cars so he utilized his hard-won mechanical and engineering skills gained during his many years of commitment to Kenya's Rhino Charge charity. Once the five cars had been delivered at the onset of filming, he was able to join Owen Newman on location for a few weeks to help find and follow the River Pride, and he quickly discovered that as much patience and determination is needed in the field as in the garage.

AMANDA BARRETT

Working in the world of natural-history filmmaking since 1987, Amanda's career with the BBC's Natural History Unit has involved writing for magazines and books, as well as crafting scripts and producing a variety of wildlife documentaries. For *African Cats*, Amanda was involved with the logistics side of the production and with following the lions as they trekked through the Masai Mara for several months at a time. As a result, she got to know the personalities of the different lions, which helped Amanda to encapsulate their actions into a thought-provoking story.

NATASHA BREED

Growing up in Kenya, "Tash" had a golden opportunity to grow up close to wildlife, leading her to work as a field assistant on programs featuring a variety of animals from army ants to elephants. Working with both Sophie and Owen, Tash followed the River Pride and Sita with great sensitivity and understanding. She became an expert not only at finding these big cats but also at reading their behavior and as a result accumulated a treasure trove of information about both characters. She also has an enviable ability to spot a leopard's tail dangling in a tree from a kilometer away.

SOPHIE DARLINGTON

Inspired by the legendary filmmaker Hugo van Lawick, Sophie studied filmmaking under the wide-open skies of Tanzania's Serengeti National Park. As a cinematographer on many of Hugo's films in the 1990s, she focused on cheetahs and lions for several films, and it was these that equipped her for following and filming Sita the cheetah for an action-packed ten months. With her creative compositions, deft use of light, and ability to follow dramatic action, Sophie played the major role in filming the story of this charismatic star.

SIMON KING

With a huge passion for wildlife, Simon is one of Britain's best-known wildlife presenters. However, wildlife filmmaking has been his other passion, and he has been making wildlife television programs since he was a teenager. He has filmed across the globe, but the Masai Mara is the place where he has filmed the most, with the big cats his prime subject. Admired for his deep understanding of animal behavior, an eye for action, and his uncanny ability to know where and when drama will unfold, Simon has captured some of the most breathtaking moments of the cheetah story.

OWEN NEWMAN

In 1979, Owen began filming and directing wildlife programs. Now, his extensive portfolio includes animals as diverse as mice, jaguars, and kangaroos. He is highly respected by the wildlife filmmaking industry for his creative, artistic, and warmly revealing animal portraits. Despite his prior experience filming the big cats, developing and filming this particular lion story was an exacting task. Patience was vital since lions are well versed in conserving their energy, but the hard-won dramatic moments have added up to an unusually emotional and gripping tale.

KEITH SCHOLEY

Keith's fascination with African cats began as a child in Kenya and continued through his zoology PhD research and later as a wildlife filmmaker. As a member and then head of the BBC Natural History Unit, he made films about African Cats and created the television series *Big Cat Diary*. He subsequently led the BBC's factual departments, returning to wildlife filmmaking in 2008 to direct and produce *African Cats*. Here, he brought together a production team with unrivaled filming experience of the Mara's big cats, creating a real-life cinema adventure.

MARGUERITE SMITS VAN OYEN

Arriving in Tanzania in 1988, Marguerite, like Sophie, learned the craft of wildlife filmmaking from Hugo van Lawick, becoming a producer and making films, many about the big cats across Africa. Afterward she teamed up with Simon King to make more films including one where they trained two orphaned cheetah cubs to go back to the wild. For *African Cats*, Marguerite concentrated on the cheetahs, supporting both Sophie and Simon, and developing the story as events unfolded. Her prior knowledge of the Mara cheetahs allowed her to identify "our" cheetahs and map out their amazing dynasty.

ACKNOWLEDGMENTS

This film would not have been made without the unwitting cooperation of a whole host of animals, from the leading characters to the arch-villains, none of whom are as clear-cut as we have, from necessity, made them out to be. We hope that our intrusion into their lives was as painless as we intended. All films also rely heavily on a solid supporting cast. Now is our chance to offer sincere thanks to the rangers, wardens, and executive officers who administer both halves of the reserve and who made our lives far easier.

Mara Conservancy and Trans Mara County Council where we thoroughly appreciated the help given by Alfred Bett, William Deed, Brian Heath, Kilgoris District Council, Joseph Kimojino, Samson Lenjirr, Wilson Naitoi, Charles Ololtele and all the other rangers who provided security and gave us much invaluable information and encouragement. In addition, going on a snare patrol opened our eyes as to how they risk their lives to safeguard the long-term future of the wildlife and ecology in the area. Their website: maratriangle.org

Masai Mara National Reserve and Narok County Council where we extend equal thanks to the Chief Warden James Sindiyo, Deputy Warden Steven Minis, and Warden Moses Kuyioni as well as the rangers and clerks who also provided security for our main camp and gave us support during the trials and tribulations of the production.

Governor's Camp provided the logistical support from August 2008 to April 2009, so many thanks to the camp staff marooned at Hammerkop as well as those based at Governor's and Little Governor's, not forgetting Patrick Beresford and his mechanics who helped keep our cars going. The driver guides, Emmanuel Kantai, Japhet Jamenya Kivango, Gideon Lempeti Kuluo, Joseph Mandila, Simon Mgorog, Josphat Munyao, Stephen Mutua, Joseph Mwangi, Jacob Ngungari, Francis Ntuala, and Philip Nzuve were instrumental in finding and following Sita and her cubs and the River Pride over many months, and enabling us to film many memorable events that, without their help, we may have missed.

Rekero Camp drew the short straw and looked after us from April 2009 to October 2010. During this period, the film crews were crossing the Mara River back and forth, generally in hot pursuit of the lions and, occasionally, the cheetahs. Gerard, Rainee, and Dudu Beaton, Jackson Looseyia, Salaash Morompi, Jonathan Raynor and all our camp staff treated such upheavals with equanimity, unfailing professionalism, and good humor. The driver guides

Charles Abuga, Martin Kasine, Sammy Nchoe, Frederick Ronko, William ole Rotiken, and Dickson Sadera often proved adept at finding "our" lions and cheetahs when so often we had failed.

At times, we needed to take to the air to film *African Cats*, and highly experienced aerial cameraman Simon Werry did a superb job in conjunction with ace helicopter pilot Ben Simpson. Simon also made it possible to mount the stabilized helicopter camera on a crane on the back of our pickup so that he and grip, Oliver Scholey, could create wonderful tracking shots, moving alongside some of our big cat stars. Meanwhile, David Breed is the most experienced filming field assistant we know. Sadly, he was only able to join us for a short time but his help was much appreciated by both Owen and Simon Werry while in the same way Chris Brennan's help was much appreciated by Sophie.

A word of thanks to safari guide Paul Kirui based at Intrepids and working for Heritage Hotels. Paul was one of the first Kenyans to gain his Gold Medal in guiding and serves as inspiration to all the other driver guides in the country. His notes shone light on the lions' story before we arrived on the scene while Jonathan Scott did likewise. Isaac Oramat and Andrew Kasura helped us find the lions on the Mara Conservancy side of the river countless times. Last but not least, heartfelt thanks to all those tourist cars that over the months stopped us and said, "Did you know that you've just driven past a lion… ?" or cheetah, or whatever.

In Nairobi, we owe an incalculable debt of gratitude to Mia Collis and Jean Hartley of Viewfinders who organized our permits, negotiated our fees, and sorted out many day-to-day tasks; Kalpesh Solanki of Filmline Ltd who adroitly got our equipment in and out of Kenya; CMC, who undertook the onerous physical job of modifying our cars; Torben Norslund, who kept the vehicles up and running in the bush; and, of course, the Ministry of Information and Communications, the Department of Immigration, the Kenya Film Commission, and the Government of Kenya, without whose support, the film wouldn't have begun.

Modern filmmaking requires *almost as much* technology as was needed to put a man on the moon. Unfortunately, few of us can keep up, but salvation was at hand in the shape of Dan Clamp, who kept everything going at base and deep in the African bush. Special thanks also to Rachel James for managing our accounts and Elly Salisbury for providing valuable production support. Meanwhile Films@59 was our UK home for the production, and so much more. Gordon Leicester and his team kept our camera kit in working order; Gina Fucci and George Panayiotou made certain that the film could be completed. Finally, Sarah Durant from The Zoological Society of London ensured that we were accurate with our scientific facts and figures.

African Cats would never have happened without **Jean-Francois Camilleri**. Having played a crucial role in the success of *March of the Penguins*, he saw the opportunity to create Disneynature. His fundamental principle was to create an environment in which filmmakers could make the best-ever wildlife films for the cinema. He has always been true to his principles and has supported all of us creatively and financially to achieve this goal. An inspiration and close friend to all in the production, Jean-Francois has done everything he could to ensure our success.

Disneynature came to **Alastair Forthergill** to spearhead its fresh commissions. Arguably the top wildlife film producer in the world, having masterminded the TV series *Blue Planet* and *Planet Earth* and the features *Deep Blue* and *Earth*, he in turn gave us the chance to start this film. His constant input as codirector to the script, story, and the ultimate creation of the *African Cats* cinematic experience has been immense.

Without turning a hair, **Jane Hamlin** organized the contracts, equipment, budget, schedules, travel, permits, and a host of other things with efficiency, speed, and great, good humor. Acting as a lifeline to the field crew, Jane dispatched replacement equipment and invaluable advice whenever it was needed; and juggled the varying needs of offices in Paris, Los Angeles, and Bristol with incomparable aplomb. Without her, the production world of *African Cats* would have been a very chaotic place indeed.

Feature films are a complex business, and **Alix Tidmarsh** has been the one to navigate us through this world. With her past experience on movies like *Deep Blue* and *Earth*, Alix was crucial in bringing us together with the resources to do the best job.

Thank you to the fantastic Disneynature team including Sten Jorgensen, Paul Baribault, and Fanny Gire.

Special thanks to our book editor, Nancy Inteli; illustrator, Jean-Paul Orpiñas; and designer, Stuart Smith, as well as Winnie Ho, Hannah Buchsbaum, David Sokol, Jennifer Eastwood, Marybeth Tregarthen, and the rest of the team at Disney Editions.

Disney
WORLDWIDE
CONSERVATION
FUND